PENGUIN BOOKS

Patrick Kavanagh: Selected Poems

Patrick Kavanagh was born in Inniskeen, County Monaghan, in 1904, the son of a cobbler-cum-small farmer. He left school at the age of thirteen, apparently destined to plough the 'stony-grey soil' rather than write about it, but 'I dabbled in verse,' he said, 'and it became my life.' He was 'discovered' by the Literary Revival veteran, AE (George Russell), in 1929 and his poems began to appear in Irish and English journals. In 1936 his first book of verse, *Ploughman and Other Poems*, was published, and in 1938 he followed this up with *The Green Fool*, an autobiography. He spent the lean years of the war in Dublin, where *The Great Hunger* was published in 1942. After the war he published the novel *Tarry Flynn* (1948) and two further collections of verse: *A Soul for Sale* (1947) and *Come Dance with Kitty Stobling* (1960). The bulk of his verse was included in his *Collected Poems*, and some of his prose in *Collected Pruse*. He died in 1967 and is buried in his native Inniskeen.

Antoinette Quinn is the author of *Patrick Kavanagh, Born-Again Romantic* (1990), a critical study of Kavanagh's poetry and prose. She has edited *The Figure in the Cave and Other Essays* by John Montague (1989) and has published many essays on modern Irish literature. She is a Fellow of Trinity College, Dublin, where she is a Senior Lecturer in the School of English.

PATRICK KAVANAGH

Selected Poems

EDITED BY ANTOINETTE QUINN

PENGUIN BOOKS

PENGUIN BOOKS

Published by the Penguin Group
Penguin Books Ltd, 80 Strand, London WC2R 0RL, England
Penguin Putnam Inc., 375 Hudson Street, New York, New York 10014, USA
Penguin Books Australia Ltd, 250 Camberwell Road, Camberwell, Victoria 3124, Australia
Penguin Books Canada Ltd, 10 Alcorn Avenue, Toronto, Ontario, Canada M4V 3B2
Penguin Books India (P) Ltd, 11 Community Centre, Panchsheel Park, New Delhi – 110 017, India
Penguin Books (NZ) Ltd, Cnr Rosedale and Airborne Roads, Albany, Auckland, New Zealand
Penguin Books (South Africa) (Pty) Ltd, 24 Sturdee Avenue, Rosebank 2196, South Africa

Penguin Books Ltd, Registered Offices: 80 Strand, London WC2R 0RL, England

www.penguin.com

First published 1996
Reprinted in Penguin Classics 2000

6

Set in Monotype Baskerville
Typeset by Datix International Limited, Bungay, Suffolk
Printed in England by Clays Ltd, St Ives plc

Contents

Patrick Kavanagh: Poetry and Independence   ix

Notes to the Introduction   xxxviii

Bibliographical Note   xli

Select Bibliography   xliii

Extract from the Author's Note to *Collected Poems*   1

POEMS

Address to an Old Wooden Gate   3

Pygmalion   4

Ploughman   4

After May   5

Tinker's Wife   5

Inniskeen Road: July Evening   6

Sanctity   7

The Hired Boy   7

Shancoduff   8

Poplar Memory   8

Plough-Horses   9

Snail   9

Memory of My Father   10

To the Man After the Harrow   11

Spraying the Potatoes   11

Stony Grey Soil   13

A Christmas Childhood   14

Art McCooey   16

The Long Garden   17

The Great Hunger   18

Lough Derg   45

Advent   66

Consider the Grass Growing	67
Peace	68
Threshing Morning	68
A Wreath for Tom Moore's Statue	70
Pegasus	71
Memory of Brother Michael	73
Bluebells for Love	74
Temptation in Harvest	75
Father Mat	77
In Memory of My Mother	82
On Raglan Road	83
No Social Conscience	84
The Paddiad	85
Spring Day	90
Ante-Natal Dream	91
Bank Holiday	92
Irish Poets Open Your Eyes	94
To be Dead	94
Kerr's Ass	95
Who Killed James Joyce?	96
Auditors In	97
Innocence	101
Epic	101
On Looking into E. V. Rieu's Homer	102
God in Woman	103
I Had a Future	104
Wet Evening in April	105
A Ballad	105
Having Confessed	106
If Ever You Go To Dublin Town	106
After Forty Years of Age	108

CONTENTS

The Rowley Mile   109
Cyrano de Bergerac   110
Intimate Parnassus   112
On Reading a Book on Common Wild Flowers 113
Narcissus and the Women   113
Irish Stew   114
Prelude   115
Nineteen Fifty-Four   118
The Hospital   119
Leaves of Grass   119
October   120
Requiem for a Mill   121
Birth   122
Question to Life   122
Come Dance with Kitty Stobling   123
Is   124
To Hell with Commonsense   125
Canal Bank Walk   126
Dear Folks   126
Song at Fifty   127
Freedom   128
Lines Written on a Seat on the Grand
    Canal, Dublin   129
The Self-Slaved   129
The One   131
Yellow Vestment   131
Love in a Meadow   132
Miss Universe   132
Winter   133
Living in the Country   134
News Item   136

CONTENTS

Mermaid Tavern   137
Literary Adventures   138
That Garage   140
The Same Again   140
Thank You, Thank You   141
In Blinking Blankness: Three Efforts   142
One Wet Summer   144
An Insult   144
Personal Problem   145

Notes   146
Glossary of Farming Terms   195
Appendix: Contents of Collections   197
Index of Titles   199
Index of First Lines   202

Patrick Kavanagh: Poetry and Independence

In 1933 two Irish poets each published a poem in praise of his dwelling: W. B. Yeats's magisterial 'Blood and the Moon', composed just before the closing decade of his life, and Patrick Kavanagh's brief *naïf* lyric 'My Room', written at the outset of his career.[1]

Home for W. B. Yeats was Thoor Ballylee, the Norman tower in County Galway which he had transformed into both a family residence and a complex imaginative symbol,[2] and which, in the wake of Irish Independence, he imperiously celebrated as a monument to the deposed Protestant Ascendancy caste with which he now identified:[3]

Blessed be this place,
More blessed still this tower;
A bloody, arrogant power
Arose from the race
Uttering, mastering it,
Rose like these walls from these
Storm-beaten cottages . . .
I declare this tower is my symbol; I declare
This winding, gyring, spiring treadmill of a stair is my ancestral stair;
That Goldsmith and the Dean, Berkeley and Burke have travelled
  there . . .

In 'My Room' Patrick Kavanagh, one of the recently decolonized rural Catholic poor, was, unwittingly, writing back from the cottage to the tower, humorously and optimistically taking stock of his cramped conditions and meagre resources:

10 by 12
And a low roof
If I stand by the side wall
My head feels the reproof.

Five holy pictures
Hang on the walls –
The Virgin and Child
St Anthony of Padua
St Patrick our own
Leo XIII
And the Little Flower.

My bed in the centre
So many things to me –
A dining table,
A writing desk,
A couch,
And a slumber palace.

My room is a musty attic
But its little window
Lets in the stars.

It would have been difficult for a reader in 1933 to predict that the obscure author of these primitive verses could ever turn such disadvantaged material circumstances to literary advantage. With hindsight, it is possible to observe that Kavanagh was already opening a 'little window' into a previously occluded lyrical space, for the Catholic underclass which constituted the majority of the Irish Free State's population had not previously considered its domestic or interior life a worthy topic for poetry.

Read together, Yeats's lines and Kavanagh's represent a post-colonial turn in Irish verse: Yeats imaginatively empowering a disempowered colonial caste and proclaiming himself its artistic and intellectual heir; Kavanagh ignoring recent political upheavals and taking his bearings in the here and now, flaunting the association between his verse and the popular iconography of Catholic Ireland, tawdry and tasteless to the eye of artistic orthodoxy.

To those who read no further, Kavanagh might have appeared a Caliban to Yeats's Prospero. And in more pessimistic moments he himself doubted his capacity to progress from the status of undereducated, impoverished yokel to the achievement of authorial authority:

> I have not the fine audacity of men
> Who have mastered the pen
> Or the purse.
> The complexes of many slaves are in my verse.
> When I straighten my shoulders to look at the world boldly
> I see talent coldly
> Damning me to stooped attrition.
> Mine was a beggar's mission.
> To dreams of beauty I should have been born blind . . .[4]

From such inauspicious beginnings, however, Patrick Kavanagh would evolve into an exemplary post-Independence poet, liberating Anglo-Irish poetry from the political role assigned to it since the middle of the nineteenth century as an agent of nationalism or cultural separatism. For the fact of Independence had not freed this poetry from its longstanding obsession with history, mythology, folklore and the translation and adaptation of Irish-language verse, from what Samuel Beckett characterized as 'the entire Celtic drill of extraversion' whereby the personal was 'happily obliterated' in the national interest.[5] With some isolated exceptions, Anglo-Irish poets were still programmed by an ethnic aesthetic.

Like Derek Walcott after him, Kavanagh exhorted his post-Independence fellow-writers to escape into a 'historyless' world, a 'world [that] began this morning', to see their surroundings with fresh eyes and to engage in an 'Adamic' naming of place.[6] 'Naming' was, for Kavanagh, a 'love-act' and 'nothing whatever is by love debarred'. Celebration of the ordinary trivia of the poet's daily milieu was to be substituted for the recycling of Gaelic literature and folklore. The affectionate portrayal of 'The everydays of nature' or 'The life of a street' was to replace totalizing, nationalist symbols of a monolithic Ireland. The rhythms and idioms of contemporary vernacular speech were to take over from the cultivation of an Hiberno-English diction and the adaptation of Gaelic poetic techniques. 'To try to be more human' was Kavanagh's exhortation to fellow-poets who were still striving to be more Irish.

Seamus Heaney has coupled Kavanagh with Yeats as the most influential figures in the modern Anglo-Irish poetic canon: Yeats, the architectural visionary, mythologist and mage, intent on constructing a well-wrought oeuvre; Kavanagh, dismissive of system or plan ('Yeatsian invention'), opting for a relaxed, casual stance, a momentary benediction of things 'common and banal'. Irish poetry needs both these antithetical modes, Heaney concludes.[7]

Despite a decade's overlap in their two careers, Yeats knew of Kavanagh only by hearsay as one of a number of Irish 'singing-birds' discovered by his friend AE (George Russell).[8] Had he lived to read Kavanagh's mature verse, he would probably have recognized in the younger writer his anti-self, and been unsurprised to find that his poetry had summoned up its 'own opposite', 'all' that he had 'handled least, least looked upon'. To Kavanagh, who embarked on the career of full-time professional writer in 1939, the year of Yeats's death, Ireland's uncrowned poet laureate was a supreme antagonist, to be admired and resisted, though he gradually realized that his aesthetic adversary was not so much Yeats as the national cultural enterprise on which Yeats's early involvement still conferred prestige.[9]

BEGINNINGS

Patrick Kavanagh was born on 21 October 1904, the son of a cobbler cum nine-acre farmer from the townland of Mucker, in the parish of Inniskeen, County Monaghan. Inniskeen, now relatively prosperous, was then an impoverished parish where '*scraidíns* of farmers' struggled to rear large families on a few hilly or boggy acres.[10] For almost thirty-five years Patrick Kavanagh lived there, working as a cobbler and farmer, attending Masses, wakes and 'hoolies', cycling the local roads, walking the fields of his farm. Unconsciously, he was gathering material for his writings like the farmer-poet described in 'Art McCooey'; unconsciously, because it was not until a couple of years before he left Inniskeen that he began to recognize the validity of his own parish as an artistic subject.

Kavanagh's formal schooling ended at age thirteen, but in the privacy of his 'wee room' in the loft of the family home he secretly pursued a literary education, reading and versifying in his spare time. Books were in scarce supply in this economically hard-pressed society and he was largely dependent on schoolbooks, such as the Royal Reader, to further his education.[11] He pored over and learned by heart some of the most anthologized passages of English poetry. However, there was nothing in the schoolbooks to suggest that 'what happen[ed] in his own fields' was 'stuff for the Muses'[12] or that his own vernacular might be a legitimate poetic diction. So in his first published poems, those submitted to a weekly newspaper competition between 1928 and 1929, he expressed his feelings of deprivation and inadequacy in metaphors and phrases remote from his own experience: he wrote about his 'heart's bare rooms', about craving wine or gold, about doors that would not 'ope' to his knocking.[13] The only time he referred to farming or included dialect in his verse was in the semi-playful 'Address to an Old Wooden Gate', printed in a local weekly newspaper, the *Dundalk Democrat*.

Kavanagh was oblivious to the existence of contemporary Irish or world literature and had never even heard of James Joyce or W. B. Yeats until 1925, when he stumbled upon the *Irish Statesman* in a newsagent's while he was attending a fair in the market town of Dundalk. From then until it folded in 1930, this weekly journal of arts and ideas edited by AE supplanted the schoolbooks as his main educational resource. By 1929, he had learned to write the kind of vague religio-rural verse that AE favoured, and three of his poems were accepted for publication, among them 'Ploughman'. Kavanagh had made his breakthrough into the world of letters. He soon became a frequent visitor to Dublin where he was befriended by other young writers such as Frank O'Connor; AE, who had a reputation for fostering new writers, lent him books and dispensed literary advice; the *Dublin Magazine* offered him a regular publishing outlet. His decorous pastoral verses also began to appear in English journals from 1931 and in 1936 *Ploughman and Other Poems* was published by Macmillan of London.

Kavanagh's first collection consists for the most part of slight apprentice offerings. 'Tinker's Wife', where an agile tinker woman scavenges among the household rubbish on a dunghill, anticipates his later fascination with the 'bits and pieces of Everyday', but the most remarkable poem in the collection is 'Inniskeen Road: July Evening' which dramatizes the poet's relationship to his parish. This sonnet focuses on the theme of community and communication, presenting the young Inniskeen poet as a socially and linguistically isolated figure, too literary to participate in the 'half-talk code' and 'wink-and-elbow language' of his young country neighbours, too honest to subscribe to orthodox poets' 'solemn talk of contemplation'. The schoolbook poetry Kavanagh had once imitated now serves a parodic purpose. By refracting his plight through Cowper's 'Verses supposed to be written by Alexander Selkirk' (1782), he playfully exaggerates his solitariness, magnifying his deserted village into a deserted island. The poem ends with an inflationary and apparently self-mocking image:

> A road, a mile of kingdom, I am king
> Of banks and stones and every blooming thing.

But is 'blooming' a slang term of dismissal or a last-minute recognition of the poetic fertility of the place he was about to reject? Willy-nilly, Kavanagh was soon to make Inniskeen his literary kingdom.

THE GREEN FOOL

Following the publication of *Ploughman and Other Poems*, Kavanagh went to London to seek literary employment and was commissioned to write *The Green Fool* (1938). This was an autobiography with an anthropological dimension, combining a portrait of the artist with a portrait of his society. The mandate to provide a narrative about small-farm life in Ulster compelled Kavanagh to confront the subject which was closest to him but which he had so far virtually ignored. Daily and seasonal farming chores, local rituals and pastimes, religious practices and superstitions, folklore and dialect, in short a way of life that he had previously considered unworthy of literary attention, now had to be registered and documented. Inniskeen is presented benignly and with affectionate innocence in the book as the best of all possible worlds: a place where life is varied and never dull and people are kindly, colourful and amusing. Kavanagh later repudiated *The Green Fool*. It was a book directed towards two metropolitan audiences: a London publisher and readership which expected Irish fictional characters to be buffoons with the gift of the gab, and a Dublin literary set which romanticized the peasant as an *echt*-Irish figure.[14] Though *The Green Fool* undoubtedly sacrifices realism in the interest of pandering to the conflicting expectations of these two kinds of reader, it does succeed in communicating the oral culture of Inniskeen, the sayings, stories, songs and proverbs with which Kavanagh was familiar from childhood. It may simplify and sanitize the way of life it celebrates, yet it also reveals a hidden Ireland.

The critical acclaim which greeted *The Green Fool* nerved Kavanagh to give up all pretence of cobbling and farming and move to Dublin to try his fortunes as a freelance writer in August 1939. It might also have tempted him to continue producing benign pastorals and perpetuating peasant stereotypes, since there was obviously a ready market for such rustic wares and a livelihood to be earned without forfeiting literary esteem. As he would later affirm, it required enormous courage to break with established artistic representations of the rural and there was no precursor to encourage him to write out of his 'Monaghanness'.[15] Kavanagh's favourite 1930s poem, 'Shancoduff' (1937), dramatizes his doubts about engaging with an unconventional poetic terrain, juxtaposing two contrary perspectives on his chosen land. The farmer-poet of

'Shancoduff' regards his bleak, hilly acres with affectionate and proud possessiveness, personifying them, metaphorically enriching and exalting them, glossing their manifest defects as virtues; to the calculating, commercially minded cattle-drovers, by contrast, the poet's cherished fields are worthless. The poem concludes ambivalently, suggesting but not confirming the farmer-poet's qualms about prizing what others despise.

BREAKING NEW GROUND

Whatever his earlier misgivings, once he had settled in Dublin Kavanagh's relationship with Inniskeen became his primary subject. In poem after poem he named the familiar sounds and sights of home: 'Mass-going feet' crunching 'the wafer-ice on the potholes', 'the sow's rooting where the hen scratches', the 'steam rising from the load' of dung, the 'barrels of blue potato-spray . . . on a headland of July'. He adopted the perspective of a child or a nostalgic adult exile to convey the magic of ordinary and often conventionally ugly rural images, transforming the yard where his mother reared hens and sows into the Garden of the Golden Apples, revisioning the townland of Mucker as Bethlehem. But his poetic relationship with Inniskeen was not solely nostalgic; he also resented the hold his home place had exerted on him for so long. In 'Stony Grey Soil' (1940) County Monaghan is personified as a scheming, deceiving woman and in a long, unfinished narrative poem, 'Why Sorrow?', the role of parish priest prevents the hero, Father Mat, from realizing his poetic vocation. Kavanagh was also drafting a novel, variously entitled *Stony Grey Soil* and *Mother and Children*, about an imaginative young man whose aspirations are stifled by life in a country parish.

Whether his mood was celebratory or condemnatory, Kavanagh was breaking new literary ground. His intimate, closely focused images of country life were a radically new departure in Irish poetry, where the tradition of peasant romanticization was at least a century old. By the late 1930s, writers could choose from among a variety of literary stereotypes of the Irish peasant: a spiritual, non-materialist figure, poor but content; a living archive of folklore and folk song; a speaker of Irish or of a colourful or lyrical Hiberno-English; a 'wise and simple man'; a wild, elemental character, roistering and fighting. The literary peasant was usually located on a west of Ireland seaboard: the Aran islands, the Connacht mainland, Sligo. Peasantry had become a nationalist property in the period preceding Independence and in the self-consciously chauvinist period that followed, in all its guises representing Ireland's cultural separateness from England. Eamon De Valera, Taoiseach since 1932, dreamed of translating a version of this cultural idealization into a social actuality, with his vision of a contented rural Ireland composed of frugal, pious, Irish-speaking, self-sufficient communities. Kavanagh, who had worked as a subsistence farmer, was acutely aware of the gulf between cultural or political fantasy and the grim struggle to wrest a livelihood from a few stony or boggy acres. By 1942 he was angry enough to expose some of the less palatable aspects of country life in the long, impassioned narrative poem that is generally considered his masterpiece, *The Great Hunger*.

Prior to this, Kavanagh's impatience with the literary romanticization of the small farmer or farm labourer had been divulged only rarely, in poems like 'The Hired Boy' (1936). What empowered him to launch a sustained challenge to misrepresentations of small-farm Ireland was his friendship with Sean O'Faolain, Frank O'Connor and Peadar O'Donnell, the group of intellectuals who launched the monthly journal the *Bell* in October 1940. From its opening number, to which Kavanagh contributed two poems, the *Bell* rang in a new era in Irish literature, proclaiming that romantic nationalism was now outdated and that it was time to document the realities of present-day Ireland.

His sense that he was in at the start of a new era in Irish literature enabled Kavanagh to turn to literary advantage what he had previously perceived as defective circumstance, cultural deprivation and social inferiority. Far from being an isolated artistic curiosity, a ploughman-poet, he realized that he identified with the Catholic small-farming and farm-labouring classes which constituted the majority of the Irish population. As the articulate spokesman of this national majority, he had the moral authority to challenge received versions of the pastoral and substitute a subversive text, what a 'peasant's left hand wrote on the page'. The solitary, self-absorbed and virtually apolitical lyricist had been converted into an ethically and socially engaged poet. Where Yeats claimed an eighteenth-century intellectual lineage that included 'Goldsmith and the Dean, Berkeley and Burke', Kavanagh selected as his eighteenth-century artistic ancestor Art McCooey, a farm-labourer poet from his native region.

THE GREAT HUNGER

The Great Hunger, which teems with images of country life at different seasons of the year and times of the day, offers a shockingly honest and comprehensive portrayal of small-farm Ireland. Ironically entitled 'The Old Peasant' on its first appearance, it gives the lie to all the stereotypes of Irish peasantry perpetrated by literary and cultural nationalism, depicting the tillage farmer as victim rather than hero. Its protagonist, Patrick Maguire, a representative subsistence farmer, is a pathetic figure, brutalized, even vegetized by a fourteen-hour working day, an elderly wifeless and childless man, who 'lives that his little fields may stay fertile', sacrificing sexuality to agricultural productivity. Taciturn, speaking only to issue orders to his workmen or swap an occasional cliché with his neighbours, Maguire is neither a purveyor of folklore and memorable phrases, nor a rumbustious, 'playboy' hero. He is timid, cautious, passive, conformist, a victim of the small-farm ethos embodied by his mother, in which success in life is measured in terms of high crop-yields, pre-marital chastity and regular attendance at Mass and confession. Outwardly respectable by these standards, Maguire is inwardly tortured with sexual frustration. The apparently virtuous Gael is revealed as an inhibited male – obsessed with sexual fantasies, secretly masturbating over the warm hearth so dear to folklorists – but also more profoundly as a disappointed man, belatedly conscious that he has let himself be cheated of the best that life has to offer.

The Great Hunger is at its most devastating in its assault on the cherished nationalist fiction of Irish spiritual ascendancy which was largely centred on peasant Ireland, a fiction that in pre-Independence days had compensated for colonial oppression and political defeat and now lent an odour of sanctity to De Valera's austere economic programme. With oracular authority Kavanagh announces the victory of materialism over spirituality in rural Ireland, opening and closing his poem with an 'apocalypse of clay', a shocking perversion of Christ's incarnation. *The Great Hunger* also establishes a vital connection between spirituality and sexuality, generally presented as conflicting forces in contemporary Irish religious discourse. Kavanagh's God is one who delights in love and lust but has been distorted into a custodian of extra-marital chastity in a land of late and infrequent marriages.

The title of *The Great Hunger* and the recurrent motif of potato-harvesting suggest a disturbing analogy between the psycho-sexual deprivation that is depopulating and devitalizing contemporary Ireland and the famine that ravaged the country in the mid nineteenth century. (*The Great Hunger* is almost a 'famine' centenary poem.) Now the potato crop flourishes but human lives are blighted; rural Ireland is a land of full bellies and unwanted wombs, its people 'hungry for life'. This evocation of small-farm Ireland as a famine-stricken, psycho-sexual wasteland is a damning indictment, utterly subverting the dominant literary and political pieties. The pieties persisted, however. Almost a year after the publication of *The Great Hunger*, De Valera made his notorious St Patrick's Day broadcast of 1943 in which he fantasized about a rural Ireland 'joyous with sounds of industry, the romping of sturdy children, the contests of athletic youths, the laughter of comely maidens; whose firesides would be the forums of the wisdom of serene old age'.

WRITING CATHOLIC IRELAND

Kavanagh's role as champion of the oppressed and misrepresented rural Catholic Irish brought him into conflict with the previous generation of Irish writers, specifically J. M. Synge, Lady Gregory and W. B. Yeats, a core grouping in what is known as the Irish Literary Revival. From the vantage point of his ethnic and class-conscious aesthetic, these esteemed predecessors were colonial rather than indigenous writers. As members of the Protestant Ascendancy they were 'totally outside the mainstream of the people's consciousness', mere onlookers and eavesdroppers on the lives of the native Catholic Irish, whereas he was an insider by virtue of experience.[16] Synge, as the Revivalist most renowned for his dramatization of peasant Ireland, was to suffer most from Kavanagh's loy. Kavanagh was clearing a space for a new, post-colonial, nativist narrative, marginalizing the hegemonic Literary Revival narrative by insisting on its minority cultural basis. Catholicism was intrinsic to his new realist aesthetic agenda and inseparable from his literary radicalism. He had embarked on a socio-literary programme of writing Catholic Ireland.

In *Lough Derg*, written in June 1942, two months after the publication of *The Great Hunger*, Kavanagh experimented with a collective and inclusive approach to the anatomy of the national Catholic psyche. The poem is based on the most prolonged and gruelling of Irish pilgrimages, the penitential sojourn on the island of Lough Derg off the coast of County Donegal. Kavanagh as cultural analyst was attracted to the island pilgrimage because it offered a microcosm of Catholic Ireland, an assembly of women and men from different social classes, from town and country, from south and north. However, *Lough Derg* lacks *The Great Hunger*'s textural density and technical mastery and he left it unrevised and unpublished. It is at its most successful and technically adventurous in its parodying and invention of prayers to catch the mindsets and preoccupations of contemporary Irish Catholics. The tones of middle-class Catholic Ireland are clearly discernible in a parodic litany where a mother prays that her son may pass the 'Intermediate' examination and her daughter 'do well at her music'; while the God to whom the poorer people turn in a series of prayers 'shaped like sonnets' is recognizable as an Irish clientist politician, a celestial county councillor or TD, who wields considerable influence in such matters as jobs and housing. *Lough Derg* represents a conscious attempt to write in 'the unwritten spaces between the lines' of previous Irish literature, to reproduce an Irish Catholic sensibility.

DE-NATIONALIZATION – CHANGING THE SYMBOLS

Kavanagh soon abdicated his role of representative Irish poet, though without surrendering his rural Catholic credentials. His swerve away from the Literary Revival persisted, but he shifted his ground significantly.

The most radical and most liberating of Kavanagh's divergences from previous Anglo-Irish literature was his somewhat belated recognition that the notion of a monolithic Ireland was itself a cultural fiction. What he alluded to as 'the myth of Ireland as a spiritual entity' and ascribed to the Literary Revival, particularly to Yeats,[17] was in fact a nationalist fiction which had persisted in Anglo-Irish poetry since the middle of the nineteenth century. In the interests of creating an imagined Irish community[18] and making common cause against English colonialism, writers downplayed sectarian, class and regional differences and constructed a totalizing symbology. The images, metaphors and rhetoric of Anglo-Irish poetry were designed to contribute to a process of collective definition. A reader encountering such verse was to be left in no doubt as to its Irish provenance. For some nationalist critics it was not sufficient that poetry should have a national signature; it must also be affiliated with an Irish-language lyrical tradition. One of the most prescriptive of such critics, the poet and Easter Rising leader Thomas MacDonagh, defined as poems in 'the Irish mode' those which had been influenced by Irish versification or the Irish way of speech or Irish music.[19]

Yeats had been centrally involved in the promotion of an ethnic literature in the early part of his career. While his oeuvre, which was never purely ethnic, went on to intensify its exploration of other philosophies and beliefs and to interrogate his own early nationalism, much Anglo-Irish home-based poetry in the decades following Independence continued to adhere to an ethnic programme. Poets such as Thomas McGreevy, who spent many years in continental Europe, and Denis Devlin and Brian Coffey, who also lived there and in North America, were open to new European and transatlantic trends; poets who chose to live in Ireland, like F. R. Higgins and Robert Farren, produced verse in 'the Irish mode' and even Austin Clarke, a highly experimental poet, kept within its technical constraints. Not all home-based poets were consciously indigenous, but so longstanding was the connection between literature and nationalism that the cult of Irishness in verse appeared canonical. As late as 1948, Farren's literary-critical study *The Course of Irish Verse* judged Anglo-Irish poetry by an ethnic criterion.[20]

In both his poetry and his literary journalism from the mid-1940s, Kavanagh was engaged in deconstructing and replacing the still dominant nationalist symbolic framework. His uncompromising hostility towards ethnicity as an aesthetic criterion is most succinctly formulated in the phrase 'Irishness is a form of anti-art'.[21]

POETRY AND PLACE

Kavanagh countered the syncretic national myth with a 'parish myth', challenging unifying symbols, such as the image of Ireland as a woman, by presenting the island as a mosaic of different regions, drawing attention to their cultural diversity, and insisting on the primacy of the local in literature. He re-evaluated the pejorative term 'parochial', defining the parochial writer as one who 'is never in any doubt about the social and artistic validity of his parish'. Parochial literature was a comic realist art which was grounded in the local, offering an affectionate, particularized portrayal of a small, intimately known community. It was inaccessible to writers of the Ascendancy caste, such as Synge, Lady Gregory and Yeats, who were outsiders to a communal local consciousness, and it was also anti-metropolitan or, rather, indifferent to the metropolis. The three writers whom he nominated as the 'great parishioners' of Irish literature – William Carleton, George Moore and James Joyce – were courageous enough to ignore Irish literary stereotypes and to represent their own rural or urban subculture authentically. That all three were Catholic writers was not fortuitous; Kavanagh's sectarian prejudice had been redirected into parochialism.

To falsify one's parish in order to make it conform with the expectations of a metropolitan audience or a powerful literary establishment was to be a 'provincial', according to Kavanagh's redefinition of that term: 'The provincial has no mind of his own; he does not trust what his eyes see until he has heard what the metropolis – towards which his eyes are turned – has to say on any subject.'[22] He himself had been a 'provincial' in *The Green Fool*, whereas his mellow, comic realist novel *Tarry Flynn* (1948) was a 'parochial' fiction.

Tarry Flynn is a portrait of the artist which focuses on the poet's love-hate relationship with his parish. Its eponymous hero, a mystical, otherworldly farmer-poet, is also an undignified comic character, dominated by his shrewd worldly-wise mother and utterly unable to cope with the machinations of an acquisitive and inquisitive local community. Inniskeen is fictionally disguised as Dargan and transported from County Monaghan to County Cavan, but the novel's autobiographical basis is deliberately exposed when three of Kavanagh's published poems are attributed to its poet hero. Whereas in Joyce's *A Portrait of the Artist as a Young Man* (1916), Stephen Dedalus leaves Ireland to forge the uncreated conscience of his race, Tarry leaves Dargan to recreate his local parish. The parochial has replaced the national as the topos of Irish writing.

Kavanagh's own departure from his native parish had almost coincided with the outbreak of the Second World War, and in his early Dublin poetry and journalism he was conscious that wartime headlines diminished the importance of everyday living. There could scarcely have been a less propitious time to engage in parochial art. The aesthetic validity of writing about small farmers' feuds in obscure townlands while a world war looms is interrogated in 'Epic' (1951), a sonnet in which Homer's authority is invoked to allay any doubts as to the legitimacy of 'local' art:

> . . . I made the *Iliad* from such
> A local row. Gods make their own importance.

While it is customarily read as a validation of the local as artistic material, 'Epic' equally reveals Kavanagh's lack of 'belief in the virtue of a place' for poetry.[23] It is the poet who confers significance, not the place. His ultimate insight into the relationship between poetry and the material world was that creativity depended on love rather than on long acquaintance. Poets may appropriate whatever endears itself to them: 'a canal-bank seat', 'a cutaway bog', 'Steps up to houses'. Parochialism had demanded that the writer be rooted in a local community so as to represent it authentically. In the late 1950s Kavanagh pronounced that 'Real roots lie in our capacity for love and its abandon'[24] and he redefined the provincial artist as one 'who lives by other people's loves'.[25] He had finally arrived at a poetic that was both inclusive and individual, substituting for an ethnic aesthetic not another tribal aesthetic but one based on affection and accessible to all.

The manifesto poem which best summarizes Kavanagh's belief in the intimate relationship between poetry and love is 'The Hospital' (1956). Here, because 'nothing whatever is by love debarred', nothing whatever, no matter how 'functional', 'plain', 'common and banal', is debarred by poetry. So 'square cubicles', 'wash basins', 'a gravelled yard', a 'main gate that was bent by a heavy lorry' take their place in the sonnet, and snoring becomes a lyrical sound. By grounding poetry in love, Kavanagh expanded its range of potential reference to include all the phenomena of the poet's contemporary world, an emancipatory strategy for a poetry that was too preoccupied with Irishness.

Parochialism, which was an outgrowth of the documentary realism promoted by the *Bell* in the 1940s, was better suited to extended fictions than to the economy of the short lyric, especially the sonnet, Kavanagh's favourite poetic medium. While it retained its polemical usefulness as an anti-nationalist, anti-metropolitan and anti-Ascendancy aesthetic, the relevance of parochialism for his own literary practice had virtually ceased after *Tarry Flynn*. Though it maintains a realist connection in its insistence on 'naming', 'The Hospital' favours a less descriptive, more minimalist art, which snatches 'the passionate transitory', rather than indulging in documentary reportage. The love of the other that motivates poetry is to be encoded, not explored. Poetry's function is 'to record love's mystery without claptrap' and rhetoric is minimized by an eroticization of naming: 'Naming these things is the love-act and its pledge.'

Brevity and spareness were features of Kavanagh's late 1950s verse: manifestos or narratives in sonnet form, short-lined couplets, lists or inventories instead of detailed description or complicated syntax. It was now enough to 'remark', to 'mention'; 'Mere notice was enough'.

HISTORY AND PERSONALITY

'The Hospital' implicitly advocates a contemporary art, whereas pre- and post-Independence Irish poetry tended to be obsessively retrospective. In their endeavour to create a literature that would be recognizably Irish though written in English, Anglo-Irish poets turned to the old Irish sagas and to Irish history, legend and folklore for symbols, characters and themes. Cuchulain, Deirdre,

Grania, Oisin and a host of other legendary and historical figures played leading roles in countless plays and lyrics. Yeats's parting injunction to Irish poets in 'Under Ben Bulben' (1939) was to 'scorn the sort now growing up' and adopt a retrospective stance:

> Cast your mind on other days
> That we in coming days may be
> Still the indomitable Irishry.

Kavanagh parodied the 'Irish poets, learn your trade' passage in which these lines occur, countermanding Yeats's instructions by urging fellow-poets to frequent the greyhound-track and familiarize themselves with working-class suburbs. From his first years in Dublin he promoted contemporaneity in literature and turned for models to poets like W. H. Auden, Stephen Spender and Dylan Thomas, whose 'fresh young attitude and vocabulary' he admired and whose verses he found to be suffused with 'the blood of life-as-it-is-lived'.[26] His anti-historicist bias is manifest in the concluding stanza of 'Memory of Brother Michael' (1944):

> Culture is always something that was,
> Something pedants can measure,
> Skull of bard, thigh of chief,
> Depth of dried-up river.
> Shall we be thus for ever?
> Shall we be thus for ever?

Even more threatening to the prevailing ethos in Irish verse was Kavanagh's conviction that poets should write from a personal perspective and not as ethnic subjects. Samuel Beckett had noted in 1934 that 'The device common to the poets of the Revival and after' was 'flight from self-awareness' and that 'self-perception' was not for them 'an accredited theme'.[27] Whereas Anglo-Irish poetry had been chiefly concerned to express racial identity, Kavanagh cultivated subjectivity and singularity in his writings. He usually cast himself in the role of hero or anti-hero, his poems frequently taking the form of an autobiography or self-portrait from as early as 'Inniskeen Road: July Evening'. The trend towards a self-centred poetry continued throughout his career, becoming even more pronounced from the beginning of the 1950s onwards. By the end of the previous decade he had perfected the persona of angular, ill-kempt, abusive rustic, disliked and feared by Dublin's males, but kind to its children and loved by its women. This persona was now projected in his verse, most notably in 'If Ever You Go To Dublin Town' (1953). A new impulse towards introspectiveness and confessionalism is also apparent in his 1950s verse: poetry is a medium for self-analysis and self-empowerment; or its theme is the creative process, 'the Muse at her toilet'. Kavanagh's column in the monthly journal *Envoy* (December 1949 – July 1951) was significantly entitled 'Diary', and here and in his own short-lived *Kavanagh's Weekly* (1952) he preached the importance of personality in art. His aesthetic of personality is flagrantly opposed to the ethnic aesthetic he detested: 'The average man requires a ready-made cloak with the clear pattern of his nation on it, for this gives the nonentity a distinction.'[28]

Far from limiting his poetry's range of reference, the habit of frank, uninhibited self-revelation, which never deserted him, reinforced its inclusiveness. The cultivation of personality resulted in a flexible, fluid poetry which could accommodate any topic from alcoholism and its side-effects ('The Same Again', 1963) to the uneasy relations between the returned native and his former neighbours ('Living in the Country', 1959).

VERNACULAR VERSE

Their mission of resistance to colonial cultural assimilation rendered Irish poets writing in English peculiarly vulnerable to Anglophone *angst*. The twentieth-century Irish poet's painful sense of having inherited a 'gapped, discontinuous' tradition has been movingly articulated by Thomas Kinsella. Only 'at two enormous removes – across a century's silence, and through an exchange of worlds' can Irish poets encounter their Gaelic forebears.[29] The

'Irish mode' based on the imitation of Gaelic poetic techniques was intended to bridge this gapped tradition. Its principal practitioner in Kavanagh's lifetime was Austin Clarke, who presented contemporary urban images and disturbing autobiographical experiences in an English diction contorted by assonance.

Kavanagh's intolerance of cultural nationalism and his unwavering focus on the contemporary left him peculiarly unsympathetic to the various linguistic devices to which Irish poets had recourse in order to emphasize their racial difference from English poets. His reaction was similar to Wole Soyinka's rebuttal of Negritude: 'a tiger does not proclaim its tigritude'. In Kavanagh's formulation 'a man is what he is, and if there is some mystical quality in the Nation or the race it will ooze through his skin'.[30] Neither did he suffer from that 'colonial cringe' in face of the dominant language of the conqueror momentarily evident in Stephen Dedalus's admission 'my soul frets in the shadow of his language'. English was for him the normal vernacular of Ireland and he experienced no postcolonial anxieties on this score; it was the Irish language which Independent Ireland was endeavouring to revive that appeared to him an 'acquired speech'.

Kavanagh believed that poetry should avoid artificial diction and express itself in a personalized vernacular. The whole thrust of his aesthetic was towards increasing freedom of speech. This was the linguistic corollary of his conviction that poetry should be inclusive and individualized. Sometimes he presented poetry as primarily an expression of personality; sometimes he compared poets to torch-holders, briefly illuminating or kindling whatever material they chanced upon.[31] Either way, poetry presented a personal 'point of view' and should communicate a sense of unique personality. Though he did still occasionally indulge in self-portraiture and reminiscence, from the early 1950s onwards Kavanagh was concerned to fashion a poetic style of utterance which would be recognizably his without the external trappings of characterization. To capture the interplay of his many inconsistent traits and tendencies, any one poem might encompass a variety of tones and moods from the condemnatory to the consoling, the cheeky to the celebratory. His vocabulary ranges from the racy and demotic to the abstruse; literary allusions jostle with everyday idioms; agricultural, suburban and biblical images mingle with those drawn from banking, the boxing ring, the betting shop, the pub, the race-track. What connects all these diverse discourses is the poem's mercurial, quizzical narrator, renewing clichés and platitudes by placing them in new and surprising contexts, setting 'an old phrase burning'. At the same time, the intersection of these different linguistic registers reveals the volatile and capricious poetic persona, who contains multitudes, who is man of the world, mystic, worshipper, ironist, voluptuary, ascetic.

Whereas Irish ethnic poetry emphasized craft, Kavanagh increasingly cultivated a casual, impromptu attitude. The tendency of his verse is towards an ever more relaxed, easy and informal manner, letting 'rip', blabbing out confidences, commenting on trivia. He took more and more liberties in verse, from the improvisatory opening lines of 'Auditors In' (1951) to the antic leaps of 'Come Dance with Kitty Stobling' (1958). The fun of the poetry usually derives from the play of incongruities through which personal idiosyncrasy is expressed in verse: juxtaposition or splicing of incompatible images, distortions of scale or perspective, parody. So commonsense is 'a bank will refuse a post Dated cheque of the Holy Ghost'; a canal lock 'niagarously roars', a neighbourhood ass is 'exiled' to Mucker; 'Who Killed James Joyce?' (1951) cues in a send-up of the Joyce industry in academia. Rhyme rather than serving as a restraint often contributes to the high jinks, its disparate couplings (purity/security, illegitimates/fates, bridges/ courageous) also serving to unite the poem's deliberately ill-assorted milieux. The answer to the double question in 'Auditors In'

> Is verse an entertainment only?
> Or is it a profound and holy
> Faith . . .

is that it is both, and, usually, simultaneously. There was a 'light verse' dimension to most of Kavanagh's serious poetry. As the punning title of 'Auditors In' indicates, he was an audience-conscious poet; a working journalist, he wrote with the expectation of being read.

POLEMICISM AND PERSONAL CIRCUMSTANCES

From his first years in Dublin onwards, Kavanagh was an embattled writer in a country in which nationalism remained the major collective passion. He condemned almost the entire previous generation of poets and dramatists, with the notable exception of AE, as colonialists in native disguise, though Yeats in spite of his Big House connections commanded his grudging respect. He was equally sweeping in his dismissal of his own generation, breaking ranks with what he referred to as 'the standing army of Irish poets'[32] because of their ethnic aesthetic. He even denounced fellow-writers with whom he had once been on friendly terms, such as Sean O'Faolain and Frank O'Connor. He was an implacable opponent of the movement to revive the Irish language, and of any institutionalization of national culture in the Free State, which became a republic in 1948. With hindsight it is possible to observe that Kavanagh's often vociferous self-dissociation from prevailing cultural tendencies in Ireland was principled and consistent with his evolving aesthetic. According to his own agricultural metaphor, he was clearing 'the ground against the crop' he 'wanted to sow'.[33] Where many of his contemporaries exemplified the trend towards essentialism or traditionalism characteristic of newly independent countries, he exemplified the typical contrary trend towards epochalism or modernity.[34] In his own time, however, though he always attracted some supporters, he was often underestimated as merely a disruptive and destructive presence, an ill-behaved boor bothering 'Ireland with muck and anger'. The state of mutual contempt in which he and his fellow-writers co-existed is dramatized in 'The Paddiad' (1949), which also illustrates the moral righteousness which he brought to the quarrel – Paddy Conscience versus the Devil.

Kavanagh suffered from the common post-colonial condition of disenchantment at the rapid solidification of a new or pre-existent middle class in a period when social mobility had seemed possible. *By Night Unstarred*, an unfinished and posthumously published novel, testifies to his envious scorn for Dublin's parvenus,[35] as do many of his satirical poems. 'Buckleppers' was his name for them. Through his own talent and determination he had elevated himself from country cobbler to London-published author only to find further upward mobility barred and livelihood itself precarious in Dublin. He hoped for patronage, a sinecure, even for regular employment, but was condemned to the uncertain economic status of a freelance journalist in a limited market, denied the middle-class trappings of 'A car, a big suburban house'. Because of the Second World War, which effectively marooned him in Dublin, eleven years elapsed between his first collection of poetry and his second, *A Soul for Sale and Other Poems* (1947). 'Pegasus' (1944), with which this volume opens, reveals his new preoccupation with the economics of being a poet.

For the next decade his anger and disappointment at Dublin's failure to reward his genius became conflated with his assault on its literary establishment. His aesthetic agenda and his promotion of his own cause were almost inseparable and though he was, undoubtedly, deserving of a hearing on both counts, his personalizing of cultural issues confused the argument and hampered critical debate. A temperamental cussedness, later exacerbated by alcoholism, the cultivation of an abrasive, uncouth persona and a terse, barbed wit, alienated many of Dublin's most intellectual and influential citizens, though he could be kindly and humorous, too, and to women was generally gallant and charming.

It might be argued that Kavanagh's predicament was that he continually needed emotional, moral and material support in his lonely crusade against the prevailing Irish poetic orthodoxies, but was at best ambivalent about the ideological compromises involved in accepting such assistance. So he acknowledged no lasting obligation to friends or donors and frequently fired on the ships that were coming to rescue him[36]. For nurture and cosseting he turned to women who, because they played little public role in the Free State or later Republic, were less politically compromised than their fathers and brothers. Yet it must also be confessed that what Kavanagh sometimes characterized as his 'kink of rectitude'[37] was a kink of self-destructiveness; he was equipped with a temperamental tripwire which he tended to activate whenever success threatened. He tested friendship to its human limits and envisaged God as a ceaselessly benevolent presence, a trusting, devoted female or a male 'who refuses / To take failure for an answer'. Nevertheless, it was his capacity for discord and feuding that allowed Kavanagh to sustain his critique of contemporary Irish cultural values and to direct so much emotional vigour into articulating an opposing aesthetic. Courage, by which he meant dissent from accepted norms, was perhaps the literary and personal quality he most admired.[38]

COMEDY

Though Kavanagh concludes his *Self-Portrait* by proclaiming that 'courage is nearly everything', it was a quality too often demonstrated through controversy and hostile confrontation. By the end of his first decade in Dublin he was conscious that he was squandering his literary energy on verse satires, flytings of his fellow-writers, and negative cultural criticism. He risked becoming permanently trapped in a pose of righteous indignation. Without calling a ceasefire then or later, he began to thematize his renunciation of a public role, his aspiration to be 'no-one's but his own saviour'. Comedy, on his definition of it, offers an alternative to crusading.

While it retains its customary connection with fun and laughter and its customary opposition to dullness and boringness, comedy, as Kavanagh defines it, is a state of mind, a point of view, conducive to creativity. The 'main feature of a poet' is 'humourosity'.[39]

To be a comic poet is to be 'passive, observing with a steady eye', uninvolved, 'not caring'; or, contrariwise, to love, delight in, be awestruck by life's passing show, and to

> praise, praise, praise
> The way it happened and the way it is.[40]

What these two apparently incompatible attitudes have in common is that neither allows for any indulgence in anger, ill-will or righteous meddling. Having identified hatred and polemicism as the enemies of creativity, Kavanagh is attempting to 'seal' his 'heart'

> From the ravening passion that will eat it out
> Till there is not one pure moment left[41]

Even his 1930s verse was not lacking in comic moments and there are many amusing twists in the complex weave of *The Great Hunger*, yet Kavanagh's recognition of the primacy of comedy in art ('all true poems laugh inwardly') was a relatively late development. The transition from negative critique to equanimity or celebration is the theme of many of his early 1950s poems. Their poet-hero, beset by pressures from within his own psyche and from without, wins through to that serene or blessed mood in which poetic composition can occur. Kavanagh subscribed to an inspirational theory about art: poetry could not be coerced or contrived but the ground could be prepared for it by the poet's cultivation of an unruffled or loving disposition. His early 1950s verse is therefore concerned with self-reform:

> And you must take yourself in hand
> And dig and ditch your authentic land[42]

An unruly, worldly, envious, greedy self is admonished to forgo its rages and its appetites so as to achieve poethood. Whereas Joyce's Stephen Dedalus left Ireland in order to 'fly by' the nets of 'nationality, language, religion', the poetic persona in Kavanagh's lyrics wishes to fly 'Away, away on wings like Joyce's' without physically going into exile. His destination is an uncontaminated psychic space or time, a 'placeless heaven', a 'positive world', a 'free moment . . . brand new and spacious' and 'beyond the reach of desire'.

Creativity in Kavanagh's 1950s lyrics is associated with nurture and affection: the muses must be constantly charmed and fed. His God is not an 'abstract Creator' but one 'who caresses the daily and nightly earth', who breathes love; Heaven is 'the generous impulse, is contented/With feeding praise to the good . . .'

Comic detachment is represented as occupying the 'high ground', being positioned on a 'tall column', on Olympus or Parnassus, or on stilts; and also, as in the Dedalus comparison, by travel and flight. 'Flight', a defiance of gravity in both its senses, is Kavanagh's image for an art that avoids being entrapped by worldly duties and obligations, that is impulsive, spontaneous and carefree. Rhyming it with another recurring image, 'light' ('flight/In the light'), accentuates its unfreighted condition as well as relating it to his belief that poetry is the expression of a personal vision or point of view, a momentary illumination, 'Nothing thought out'.

Comedy is, paradoxically, both caring and uncaring. It cherishes particular scenes and treasures particular moments but refuses political or social involvement. So Kavanagh repudiated *The Great Hunger* because it was 'concerned with the woes of the poor' and denounced it as a tragedy: '*The Great Hunger* is tragedy and Tragedy is underdeveloped Comedy, not fully born.'[43]

POETRY AND IRRESPONSIBILITY

By 1964, when he condemned his own early masterpiece, Kavanagh was opposed to all programmatic art. His 'purpose in life was to have no purpose'. In a country where literature had been imbricated in nationalism for over a century, he was asserting art's right to remain aloof and disengaged: 'The heart of a song singing it, or a poem writing it, is not caring.' His own ultimate achievement, as he perceived it, was to have arrived 'at complete casualness, at being able to play a true note on a dead slack string'.[44] As well as abrogating political or social responsibility, Kavanagh was here reiterating his advocacy of an art that conceals art and his antipathy to the notion of an oeuvre. The poet gathers, collects, the 'bits and pieces' that take his fancy rather than working to some formula or preconceived plan. Yet he was not prepared to sacrifice intensity; the obverse of the positive action of gathering is the negative ('hellish') one of scattering.

In his insistence on presenting poetry as 'a way of saying' or a way of seeing, rather than a social or political document, Kavanagh was not only severing the link between literature and nationalism. He was suppressing the enemy within, the dogmatist in himself. For all his lauding of Parnassian or Olympian remoteness and unconcern, his promotion of passivity, of 'watching' or wallowing as the proper poetic activities, his view that poetry should be 'airborne' and 'weightless', he is a doctrinaire poet. His cultural and literary critique and his poetry are almost inextricably linked and his lyrics are rarely innocent of their aesthetic politics. Some are literary credos or manifestos and many include pronouncements about his own poetry or poetry in general. Gaiety or flippancy in his verse expresses a serious intent; a poem like 'To Hell with Commonsense' (1958) is irreverent but didactic. As his comment on 'purpose', above, reveals, for him even purposelessness is purposeful. Irresponsibility ultimately eludes him because he cannot cease caring passionately about poetry itself.

A pivotal event in Kavanagh's career as a poet was his operation for lung cancer in March 1955, or, rather, the later phase of the convalescence that followed. In the warm July of that year he lay weakened and idle on the grassy bank of the Grand Canal day after day, grateful to have been granted a further lease of life and keenly appreciative of the most 'common and banal' objects in his vicinity. He was at last enjoying the comic experience his poetry had so long desiderated. He declared himself not merely physically and psychically healed, but born again and rebaptized in canal water, a new, ebullient, zanily happy poet with an 'inexhaustible' wealth of material at his command. The poet figure in his late 1950s verse is euphoric, exuberant, maniacally delighted to be alive, and the verse consists of rhapsodic love poems and hymns to the world, to canal and street as well as to summer lane and cutaway bog. *Come Dance with Kitty Stobling*, the title of his award-winning 1960 collection,[45] catches something of the exhilaration and ludic energy of this late phase in Kavanagh's verse.

In the final years of his life Kavanagh struggled with alcoholism, failing health and waning creativity. However, the inclusive, personal and casual poetic he had evolved enabled him to versify such distressing circumstances. Where he had turned to W. H. Auden to modernize his poetry at the outset of his Dublin career, he was now excited by the fun and games of Beat verse which could relieve poetry of 'ponderosity'.[46] 'Let words laugh' he wrote in 'Mermaid Tavern' (1962). In practice, this could result in a playful emphasis on rhyme and sometimes a descent into doggerel. Carefreeness easily degenerated into carelessness. Yet the technique of casualness which he had been cultivating throughout the 1950s is peculiarly appropriate to these final confessional poems, bringing a tone of comic ruefulness to their sorry tale of alcoholic indignity and poetic disability. Kavanagh has at last shed his 'messianic compulsion',[47] the conception of the poet as 'prophet and saviour', for which his role models were AE and W. B. Yeats, the dominant Literary Revival figures at the start of his own poetic odyssey. His late poems endeavour to admit the whole adult man into poetry, not to compartmentalize the satirist and the celebrant or seek to purify the grouchy, opportunistic aspects of the self (as in 'Living in the Country', 1959). 'The way it happened and the way it is' are rarely glamorized and happy endings are few.

In Kavanagh's own life there were many rewards before the end came on 30 November 1967: an admiring and supportive new generation of Irish poets, critical acclaim in England, a steady demand for his literary services, the publication of his *Collected Poems* (1964) and *Collected Pruse* (1967), marriage[48] – much for which to say 'Thank You, Thank You':

> For most have died the day before
> The opening of that holy door.

Patrick Kavanagh summoned Anglo-Irish poetry out of a protracted Celtic twilight into the more confusing light of contemporary day. His achievement is to have transformed the symbolic framework within which that poetry operated. The aftershock of his assault on the ethnicity which had dominated Anglo-Irish verse since the mid nineteenth century was still being registered as late as 1965 when the poet John Montague, acknowledging the liberating honesty of Kavanagh's vision, declared, 'it has liberated us into ignorance'.[49] Anglo-Irish poetry had been decolonized, but, deprived of a national role, it was bereft of its principal themes and topics and had everything to learn. Kavanagh's emancipatory legacy to Irish poets is to steer clear of tribalism and politico-cultural responsibility, to trust the pull of personal impulses and affections and refuse to be daunted by the apparent inadequacies of their own situation, to 'wallow in the habitual, the banal' aspects of contemporary life, and to write an unashamedly vernacular verse:

> O Come all ye gallant poets – to know it doesn't matter
> Is Imagination's message – break out but do not scatter.
> Ordinary things wear lovely wings – the peacock's body's common.
> O Come all ye youthful poets and try to be more human.[50]

Notes to the Introduction

1. 'Blood and the Moon', first published in *The Exile* in spring 1928, was collected in *The Winding Stair and Other Poems*, London, 1933; 'My Room' first appeared in the *Dublin Magazine*, April–June 1933.

2. Thoor Ballylee was Yeats's summer residence between 1919 and 1929.

3. The Irish Free State was established in 1922; the Protestant Ascendancy constituted the ruling class in Ireland from 1697 until 1922.

4. 'The Irony of It', the *Irish Times*, 14 February 1938.

5. *The Bookman*, August 1934, under the pseudonym Andrew Belis.

6. 'The Muse of History', *Is Massa Day Dead? Black Moods in the Caribbean*, ed. Orde Coombes, New York, 1974, pp. 1–27.

7. 'Unhappy and at Home', interview with Seamus Heaney by Seamus Deane, *The Crane Bag*, 1, i, 1977.

8. *Letters to W. B. Yeats*, vol. 2, ed. Richard J. Finneran, George Mills Harper, William M. Murphy, London, 1977, pp. 533 and 547–8.

9. For a more detailed discussion of Kavanagh's ambivalent attitude to Yeats, see my *Patrick Kavanagh, Born-Again Romantic*, Dublin and New York, 1991.

10. Based on Kavanagh's account in *Self-Portrait*, Dublin, 1964, p. 9.

11. In the *Irish Times*, 11 April 1940, Kavanagh tells how as a young man he discovered the sixth book of the Royal Reader, a discarded school textbook, in the smoky nook of a neighbour's chimney. There he read for the first time such poems as Dryden's 'A Song for St Cecilia's Day', Goldsmith's 'The Deserted Village' and Keats's 'Endymion' and 'Ode to a Nightingale'.

12. Daniel Corkery in *Synge and Anglo-Irish Literature*, Cork, 1931, p. 15, pointing out how the Irish writer was disadvantaged by a colonial education.

13. The *Irish Weekly Independent* offered a weekly prize of half a guinea for the best contribution to its poetry column, 'A Selection of Irish Verse'. Kavanagh never won the prize but as a runner-up had his verse published on fifteen occasions between 1 September 1928 and 8 June 1929.

14. *Self-Portrait*, p. 7.

15. 'Return in Harvest', the *Bell*, April 1954; see also 'From Monaghan to the Grand Canal', *Studies*, spring 1959.

16. The *Standard*, 28 May 1943; see also the *Bell*, February 1951. For a fuller discussion of Kavanagh's critique of Synge, Gregory and Yeats, see *Patrick Kavanagh, Born-Again Romantic*, especially pp. 166–70 and 196–8.

17. According to *Self-Portrait*, p. 11, the 'notion' that Ireland was 'a spiritual entity' was 'invented and patented by Yeats, Lady Gregory and Synge'.

18. Based on Benedict Anderson, *Imagined Communities*, London, 1983.

19. *Literature in Ireland*, Dublin, 1916, pp. 64–103 and 178–219.

20. Kavanagh's review of this book was so scathing that the *Irish Times* refused to publish it.

21. *Self-Portrait*, p. 14.

22. The quotations on 'parochialism' and 'provincialism' are all from *Kavanagh's Weekly*, 24 May 1952. For a fuller discussion of Kavanagh's views, see *Patrick Kavanagh, Born-Again Romantic*, pp. 195–253.

23. *Self-Portrait*, pp. 14–15.

24. 'From Monaghan to the Grand Canal'.

25. *November Haggard*, ed. Peter Kavanagh, New York, 1971, p. 69.

26. 'Liberators', the *Irish Times*, 15 August 1942.

27. 'Recent Irish Poetry', *The Bookman*, August 1934.

28. *Kavanagh's Weekly*, 7 June 1952.

29. W. B. Yeats and Thomas Kinsella, *Davis, Mangan, Ferguson? Tradition and the Irish Writer*, Dublin, 1970, pp. 57–66.

30. 'The Gallivanting Poet', *Irish Writing*, November 1947.

31. 'Auden and the Creative Mind', *Envoy*, June 1951; 'From Monaghan to the Grand Canal'.

32. *Collected Poems*, London, 1964, p. 114.

33. 'Diary', *Envoy*, September 1950.

34. The post-colonial analysis here and in the next paragraph is based on Clifford Geertz, *The Interpretation of Cultures*, London, 1975, pp. 234–54. The terms 'essentialism' and 'epochalism' are Geertz's.

35. *By Night Unstarred*, the Curragh (Ireland), 1977.

36. ibid., p. 126.

37. 'From Monaghan to the Grand Canal'.

38. 'Diary', *Envoy*, June 1950; see also *Self-Portrait*, p. 30.

39. *Self-Portrait*, p. 24

40. 'Question to Life', *Time and Tide*, 12 April 1958.

41. 'On Reading a Book on Common Wildflowers', the *Bell*, March 1954.

42. 'Auditors In', the *Bell*, October 1951.

43. 'Author's Note', *Collected Poems*.

44. *Self-Portrait*, pp. 23 and 29.

45. It was the Poetry Book Society's summer choice in 1960.

46. *Hibernia*, May 1964; see also *Tri-quarterly*, 4, 1965.

47. 'Author's Note', *Collected Poems*.

48. He married Katherine Barry Maloney on 19 April 1967.

49. John Montague, 'Patrick Kavanagh: A Speech from the Dock', *The Figure in the Cave and Other Essays*, ed. Antoinette Quinn, Dublin, 1989, p. 142.

50. 'Spring Day', *Envoy*, March 1950.

Bibliographical Note

Selected Poems is largely based on Patrick Kavanagh's *Collected Poems* (1964), though it differs markedly from that collection. Some poems not collected in 1964 have been added, most notably *Lough Derg*. Some poems collected in 1964 have been omitted, in particular, from Kavanagh's first collection, *Ploughman and Other Poems* (1936), from the satires (1944–54) and from the later poems (1960–67). *Selected Poems* is also differently organized from *Collected Poems*. The poems are printed in order of first publication as far as possible and, in the case of several poems taken from one source text, in the order that they appear within that collection. In the case of *Lough Derg*, which was published posthumously, the placing is determined by the date of composition. This ordering was chosen both to accommodate poetry not collected in Kavanagh's lifetime and because the lengthy interval between his collections – *Ploughman and Other Poems* (1936), *A Soul for Sale and Other Poems* (1947) and *Come Dance with Kitty Stobling and other Poems* (1960) (which includes some pre-1947 material) – makes it difficult to follow the trajectory of the poet's career.

Since *Collected Poems* is blemished by misprints, I have not normally used it as the source text of *Selected Poems*. Instead, I have returned to the volume in which the poems were previously collected, or, in the case of previously uncollected published poems, to their first publication. *The Great Hunger*, however, follows the original Cuala Press edition of 1942 and not the bowdlerized version printed in *A Soul for Sale*. In the case of poems which were not published in Kavanagh's lifetime, such as *Lough Derg*, I have followed the manuscript version. The source text and, where applicable, the date and place of first publication of each poem are stated in the Notes at the end of the book.

While each source text has been faithfully reproduced in this edition, certain spellings have been standardized/modernized throughout (e.g. 'tonight'/'tomorrow' instead of 'to-night'/'to-morrow'; 'ninety-one' instead of 'ninety one') and, very occasionally, alterations have been made to punctuation (e.g. a full stop supplied where one is clearly missing), especially in the case of *Lough Derg* which is taken from the original typescript. Where misprints have been amended in the original text, this is commented upon in the Notes.

As regards the selection in this book, I have preserved what I consider to be Kavanagh's best verse, but I have also included some inferior verse because it represents a particular phase or propensity in his oeuvre. I have also attempted to balance the claims of new readers and those well acquainted with Kavanagh's poetry who will resent the exclusion of familiar poems. In the interests of newcomers, his 1930s verse has been curtailed so that they will encounter his mature verse early in the book. Such readers have also been spared some of the satires which Kavanagh himself did not care to collect and the late verse he did not bother to publish. For the sake of that other readership, whom Kavanagh would have called his *affectionados*, many of whom like myself were reared on *Collected Poems*, I have retained quite a few poems which a more rigorous selector might have jettisoned.

I trust that my prefacing of the *Selected Poems* with an extract from the Author's Note in *Collected Poems* will be taken in the spirit it is intended, as an acknowledgement of the poet's own perspective on his poetry, rather than a presumption of his blessing on the present collection.

Select Bibliography

PRIMARY SOURCES

Books

Ploughman and Other Poems, Macmillan, London, 1936.

The Green Fool (1938), Penguin Books, Harmondsworth, 1975.

The Great Hunger, the Cuala Press, Dublin, 1942. Facsimile edition, Irish University Press, Shannon, 1971.

A Soul for Sale and Other Poems, Macmillan, London, 1947.

Tarry Flynn (1948), Penguin Books, Harmondsworth, 1978.

Recent Poems, the Peter Kavanagh Hand Press, New York, 1958.

Come Dance with Kitty Stobling and Other Poems, Longmans, Green and Co., London, 1960.

Collected Poems, MacGibbon and Kee, London, 1964.

Self-Portrait, the Dolmen Press, Dublin, 1964.

Collected Pruse, MacGibbon and Kee, London, 1967.

November Haggard, 'Uncollected Prose and Verse of Patrick Kavanagh', ed. Peter Kavanagh, the Peter Kavanagh Hand Press, New York, 1971.

The Complete Poems, ed. Peter Kavanagh, the Peter Kavanagh Hand Press, New York, 1972.

By Night Unstarred, ed. Peter Kavanagh, the Goldsmith Press, the Curragh (Ireland), 1977.

Lough Derg, Martin, Brian and O'Keeffe, London, 1978, and the Goldsmith Press, the Curragh (Ireland), 1978.

Manuscripts

The Kavanagh Archive is in the library of University College, Dublin. There are also manuscripts and other documents in the National Library of Ireland and Trinity College Library, Dublin.

SELECT BIBLIOGRAPHY

SECONDARY SOURCES

Lapped Furrows: Correspondence 1933–1967 between Patrick and Peter Kavanagh with Other Documents, ed. Peter Kavanagh, the Peter Kavanagh Press, New York, 1971.

Alan Warner, *Clay is the Word*, the Dolmen Press, Dublin, 1973.

D'Arcy O'Brien, *Patrick Kavanagh*, Bucknell University Press, Lewisburg, 1975.

John Ryan, *Remembering How We Stood*, Gill and Macmillan, Dublin, 1975.

Anthony Cronin, *Dead as Doornails*, the Dolmen Press, Dublin, 1976.

John Nemo (ed.), *The Journal of Irish Literature*, 'a Patrick Kavanagh Number', January 1977.

Peter Kavanagh, *Sacred Keeper*, the Goldsmith Press, the Curragh (Ireland), 1979. A biography of Patrick Kavanagh.

John Nemo, *Patrick Kavanagh*, Twayne, Boston (Mass.), 1979.

Michael O'Loughlin, *After Kavanagh*, Raven Arts Press, Dublin, 1985.

Peter Kavanagh (ed.), *Patrick Kavanagh: Man and Poet*, the Goldsmith Press, the Curragh (Ireland), 1987.

Antoinette Quinn, *Patrick Kavanagh, Born-Again Romantic*, Gill and Macmillan, Dublin, and Syracuse University Press, New York, 1991.

Extract from the Author's Note to
Collected Poems

I have never been much considered by the English critics. I suppose I shouldn't say this. But for many years I have learned not to care, and I have also learned that the basis of literary criticism is usually the ephemeral. To postulate even semi-absolute standards is to silence many lively literary men.

I would not object if some critic said I wasn't a poet at all. Indeed, trying to think of oneself as a poet is a peculiar business. What does it feel like to be a poet?

I am always shy of calling myself a poet and I wonder much at those young men and sometimes those old men who boldly declare their poeticality. If you ask them what they are, they say: Poet.

There is, of course, a poetic movement which sees poetry materialistically. The writers of this school see no transcendent nature in the poet; they are practical chaps, excellent technicians. But somehow or other I have a belief in poetry as a mystical thing, and a dangerous thing.

A man (I am thinking of myself) innocently dabbles in words and rhymes and finds that it is his life. Versing activity leads him away from the paths of conventional unhappiness. For reasons that I have never been able to explain, the making of verses has changed the course of one man's destiny. I could have been as happily unhappy as the ordinary countryman in Ireland. I might have stayed at the same moral age all my life. Instead of that, poetry made me a sort of outcast. And I was abnormally normal.

I do not believe in sacrifice and yet it seems I was sacrificed. I must avoid getting too serious.

I belong to neither of the two kinds of poet commonly known. There is the young chap who goes to school and university, is told by lecturers of the value of poetry, and there is the other kind whom we somehow think inspired. Lisping in numbers like Dylan Thomas, Burns, etc.

Looking back, I see that the big tragedy for the poet is poverty. I had no money and no profession except that of small farmer. And I had the misfortune to live the worst years of my life through a period when there were no Arts Councils, Foundations, Fellowships for the benefit of young poets.

On many occasions I literally starved in Dublin. I often borrowed a 'shilling for the gas' when in fact I wanted the coin to buy a chop. During the war, in Dublin, I did a column of gossip for a newspaper at four guineas a week.

I suppose when I come to think of it, if I had a stronger character, I might have done well enough for myself. But there was some kink in me, put there by Verse.

In 1942 I wrote *The Great Hunger*. Shortly after it was published a couple of hefty lads came to my lonely shieling on Pembroke Road. One of them had a copy of the poem behind his back. He brought it to the front and he asked me, 'Did you write that?' He was a policeman. It may seem shocking to the devotee of liberalism if I say that the police were right. For a poet in his true detachment is impervious to policemen. There is something wrong with a work of art, some kinetic vulgarity in it when it is visible to policemen.

The Great Hunger is concerned with the woes of the poor. A true poet is selfish and implacable. A poet merely states the position and does not care whether his words change anything or not. *The Great Hunger* is tragedy and Tragedy is underdeveloped Comedy, not fully born. Had I stuck to the tragic thing in *The Great Hunger* I would have found many powerful friends.

But I lost my messianic compulsion. I sat on the bank of the Grand Canal in the summer of 1955 and let the water lap idly on the shores of my mind. My purpose in life was to have no purpose. . . .

Address to an Old Wooden Gate

Battered by time and weather; scarcely fit
For firewood; there's not a single bit
Of paint to hide those wrinkles, and such scringes
Break hoarsely on the silence – rusty hinges:
A barbed wire clasp around one withered arm
Replaces the old latch, with evil charm.
That poplar tree you hang upon is rotten,
And all its early loveliness forgotten.
This gap ere long must find another sentry
If the cows are not to roam the open country.
They'll laugh at you, Old Wooden Gate, they'll push
Your limbs asunder, soon, into the slush.
Then I will lean upon your top no more
To muse, and dream of pebbles on a shore,
Or watch the fairy-columned turf-smoke rise
From white-washed cottage chimneys heaven-wise.
Here have I kept fair tryst, and kept it true,
When we were lovers all, and you were new;
And many a time I've seen the laughing-eyed
Schoolchildren, on your trusty back astride.
But Time's long silver hand has touched our brows,
And I'm the scorned of women – you of cows.
How can I love the iron gates which guard
The fields of wealthy farmers? They are hard,
Unlovely things, a-swing on concrete piers –
Their finger-tips are pointed like old spears.
But you and I are kindred, Ruined Gate,
For both of us have met the self-same fate.

Pygmalion

I saw her in a field, a stone-proud woman
Hugging the monster Passion's granite child,
Engirdled by the ditches of Roscommon,
Stone ditches round her waist like serpents coiled.
Her lips were frozen in the signature
Of Lust, her hair was set eternally,
No Grecian goddess, for her face was poor,
A twisted face, like Hardship's face to me.
And who she was I queried every man
From Ballahedreen to grassy Boyle
And all replied: a stone Pygmalion
Once lipped to grey terrific smile.
I said: At dawn tomorrow she will be
Clay-sensuous. But they only smiled at me.

Ploughman

I turn the lea-green down
Gaily now,
And paint the meadow brown
With my plough.

I dream with silvery gull
And brazen crow.
A thing that is beautiful
I may know.

Tranquillity walks with me
And no care.
O, the quiet ecstasy
Like a prayer.

I find a star-lovely art
In a dark sod.
Joy that is timeless! O heart
That knows God!

After May

May came, and every shabby phoenix flapped
A coloured rag in lieu of shining wings;
In school bad manners spat and went unslapped –
Schoolmistress Fancy dreamt of other things.
The lilac blossomed for a day or two
Gaily, and then grew weary of her fame.
Plough-horses out on grass could now pursue
The pleasures of the very mute and tame.

A light that might be mystic or a fraud
Played on far hills beyond all common sight,
And some men said that it was Adam's God
As Adam saw before the Apple-bite.
Sweet May is gone, and now must poets croon
The praises of a rather stupid June.

Tinker's Wife

I saw her amid the dunghill debris
Looking for things
Such as an old pair of shoes or gaiters.
She was a young woman,
A tinker's wife.

Her face had streaks of care
Like wires across it,
But she was supple
As a young goat
On a windy hill.

She searched on the dunghill debris,
Tripping gingerly
Over tin canisters
And sharp-broken
Dinner plates.

Inniskeen Road: July Evening

The bicycles go by in twos and threes –
There's a dance in Billy Brennan's barn tonight,
And there's the half-talk code of mysteries
And the wink-and-elbow language of delight.
Half-past eight and there is not a spot
Upon a mile of road, no shadow thrown
That might turn out a man or woman, not
A footfall tapping secrecies of stone.

I have what every poet hates in spite
Of all the solemn talk of contemplation.
Oh, Alexander Selkirk knew the plight
Of being king and government and nation.
A road, a mile of kingdom, I am king
Of banks and stones and every blooming thing.

Sanctity

To be a poet and not know the trade,
To be a lover and repel all women;
Twin ironies by which great saints are made,
The agonizing pincer-jaws of Heaven.

The Hired Boy

Let me be no wiser than the dull
And leg-dragged boy who wrought
For John Maguire in Donaghmoyne
With never a vain thought
For fortune waiting round the next
Blind turning of Life's lane;
In dreams he never married a lady
To be dreamed-divorced again.

He knew what he wanted to know –
How the best potatoes are grown
And how to put flesh on a York pig's back
And clay on a hilly bone.
And how to be satisfied with the little
The destiny masters give
To the beasts of the tillage country –
To be damned and yet to live.

Shancoduff

My black hills have never seen the sun rising,
Eternally they look north towards Armagh.
Lot's wife would not be salt if she had been
Incurious as my black hills that are happy
When dawn whitens Glassdrummond chapel.

My hills hoard the bright shillings of March
While the sun searches in every pocket.
They are my Alps and I have climbed the Matterhorn
With a sheaf of hay for three perishing calves
In the field under the Big Forth of Rocksavage.

The sleety winds fondle the rushy beards of Shancoduff
While the cattle-drovers sheltering in the Featherna Bush
Look up and say: 'Who owns them hungry hills
That the water-hen and snipe must have forsaken?
A poet? Then by heavens he must be poor.'
I hear and is my heart not badly shaken?

Poplar Memory

I walked under the autumned poplars that my father
    planted
On a day in April when I was a child
Running beside the heap of suckers
From which he picked the straightest, most promising.

My father dreamt forests, he is dead –
And there are poplar forests in the waste-places
And on the banks of drains.

When I look up
I see my father
Peering through the branched sky.

Plough-Horses

Their glossy flanks and manes outshone
The flying splinters of the sun.

The tranquil rhythm of that team
Was as slow-flowing meadow stream.

And I saw Phidias' chisel there –
An ocean stallion, mountain mare,

Seeing, with eyes the Spirit unsealed
Plough-horses in a quiet field.

Snail

I go from you, I recede
Not by steps violent
But as a snail backing
From the lewd finger of humanity.

I go from you as a snail
Into my twisted habitation.

And you!
It does not matter how you
React. I know the shadow-ways
Of Self
I know the last sharp bend
And the volleyed light.

9

You are lost
You can merely chase the silver I have let
Fall from my purse,
You follow silver
And not follow me.

Memory of My Father

Every old man I see
Reminds me of my father
When he had fallen in love with death
One time when sheaves were gathered.

That man I saw in Gardner Street
Stumble on the kerb was one,
He stared at me half-eyed,
I might have been his son.

And I remember the musician
Faltering over his fiddle
In Bayswater, London,
He too set me the riddle.

Every old man I see
In October-coloured weather
Seems to say to me:
'I was once your father.'

To the Man After the Harrow

Now leave the check-reins slack,
The seed is flying far today –
The seed like stars against the black
Eternity of April clay.

This seed is potent as the seed
Of knowledge in the Hebrew Book,
So drive your horses in the creed
Of God the Father as a stook.

Forget the men on Brady's hill.
Forget what Brady's boy may say
For destiny will not fulfil
Unless you let the harrow play.

Forget the worm's opinion too
Of hooves and pointed harrow-pins,
For you are driving your horses through
The mist where Genesis begins.

Spraying the Potatoes

The barrels of blue potato-spray
Stood on a headland of July
Beside an orchard wall where roses
Were young girls hanging from the sky.

The flocks of green potato-stalks
Were blossom spread for sudden flight,
The Kerr's Pinks in a frivelled blue,
The Arran Banners wearing white.

And over that potato-field
A lazy veil of woven sun.
Dandelions growing on headlands, showing
Their unloved hearts to everyone.

And I was there with the knapsack sprayer
On the barrel's edge poised. A wasp was floating
Dead on a sunken briar leaf
Over a copper-poisoned ocean.

The axle-roll of a rut-locked cart
Broke the burnt stick of noon in two.
An old man came through a corn-field
Remembering his youth and some Ruth he knew.

He turned my way. 'God further the work.'
He echoed an ancient farming prayer.
I thanked him. He eyed the potato-drills.
He said: 'You are bound to have good ones there.'

We talked and our talk was a theme of kings,
A theme for strings. He hunkered down
In the shade of the orchard wall. O roses
The old man dies in the young girl's frown.

And poet lost to potato-fields,
Remembering the lime and copper smell
Of the spraying barrels he is not lost
Or till blossomed stalks cannot weave a spell.

Stony Grey Soil

O stony grey soil of Monaghan
The laugh from my love you thieved;
You took the gay child of my passion
And gave me your clod-conceived.

You clogged the feet of my boyhood
And I believed that my stumble
Had the poise and stride of Apollo
And his voice my thick-tongued mumble.

You told me the plough was immortal!
O green-life-conquering plough!
Your mandril strained, your coulter blunted
In the smooth lea-field of my brow.

You sang on steaming dunghills
A song of cowards' brood,
You perfumed my clothes with weasel itch,
You fed me on swinish food.

You flung a ditch on my vision
Of beauty, love and truth.
O stony grey soil of Monaghan
You burgled my bank of youth!

Lost the long hours of pleasure
All the women that love young men.
O can I still stroke the monster's back
Or write with unpoisoned pen

His name in these lonely verses
Or mention the dark fields where
The first gay flight of my lyric
Got caught in a peasant's prayer.

Mullahinsha, Drummeril, Black Shanco –
Wherever I turn I see
In the stony grey soil of Monaghan
Dead loves that were born for me.

A Christmas Childhood

[I]

One side of the potato-pits was white with frost –
How wonderful that was, how wonderful!
And when we put our ears to the paling-post
The music that came out was magical.

The light between the ricks of hay and straw
Was a hole in Heaven's gable. An apple tree
With its December-glinting fruit we saw –
O you, Eve, were the world that tempted me

To eat the knowledge that grew in clay
And death the germ within it! Now and then
I can remember something of the gay
Garden that was childhood's. Again

The tracks of cattle to a drinking-place,
A green stone lying sideways in a ditch
Or any common sight the transfigured face
Of a beauty that the world did not touch.

[II]

My father played the melodion
Outside at our gate;
There were stars in the morning east
And they danced to his music.

Across the wild bogs his melodion called
To Lennons and Callans.
As I pulled on my trousers in a hurry
I knew some strange thing had happened.

Outside in the cow-house my mother
Made the music of milking;
The light of her stable-lamp was a star
And the frost of Bethlehem made it twinkle.

A water-hen screeched in the bog,
Mass-going feet
Crunched the wafer-ice on the pot-holes,
Somebody wistfully twisted the bellows wheel.

My child poet picked out the letters
On the grey stone,
In silver the wonder of a Christmas townland,
The winking glitter of a frosty dawn.

Cassiopeia was over
Cassidy's hanging hill,
I looked and three whin bushes rode across
The horizon – the Three Wise Kings.

An old man passing said:
'Can't he make it talk' –
The melodion. I hid in the doorway
And tightened the belt of my box-pleated coat.

I nicked six nicks on the door-post
With my penknife's big blade –
There was a little one for cutting tobacco.
And I was six Christmases of age.

My father played the melodion,
My mother milked the cows,
And I had a prayer like a white rose pinned
On the Virgin Mary's blouse.

Art McCooey

I recover now the time I drove
Cart-loads of dung to an outlying farm –
My foreign possessions in Shancoduff –
With the enthusiasm of a man who sees life simply.

The steam rising from the load is still
Warm enough to thaw my frosty fingers.
In Donnybrook in Dublin ten years later
I see that empire now and the empire builder.

Sometimes meeting a neighbour
In country love-enchantment,
The old mare pulls over to the bank and leaves us
To fiddle folly where November dances.

We wove our disappointments and successes
To patterns of a town-bred logic:
'She might have been sick . . . No, never before,
A mystery, Pat, and they all appear so modest.'

We exchanged our fool advices back and forth:
'It easily could be their cow was calving,
And sure the rain was desperate that night.' . . .
Somewhere in the mists a light was laughing.

We played with the frilly edges of reality
While we puffed our cigarettes;
And sometimes Owney Martin's splitting yell
Would knife the dreamer that the land begets.

'I'll see you after Second Mass on Sunday.'
'Right-o, right-o.' The mare moves on again.
A wheel rides over a heap of gravel
And the mare goes skew-ways like a blinded hen.

Down the lane-way of the poplar banshees
By Paddy Bradley's; mud to the ankles;
A hare is grazing in Mat Rooney's meadow;
Maggie Byrne is prowling for dead branches.

Ten loads before tea-time. Was that the laughter
Of the evening bursting school?
The sun sinks low and large behind the hills of Cavan,
A stormy-looking sunset. 'Brave and cool.'

Wash out the cart with a bucket of water and a wangel
Of wheaten straw. Jupiter looks down.
Unlearnedly and unreasonably poetry is shaped
Awkwardly but alive in the unmeasured womb.

The Long Garden

It was the garden of the golden apples,
A long garden between a railway and a road,
In the sow's rooting where the hen scratches
We dipped our fingers in the pockets of God.

In the thistly hedge old boots were flying sandals
By which we travelled through the childhood skies,
Old buckets rusty-holed with half-hung handles
Were drums to play when old men married wives.

The pole that lifted the clothes-line in the middle
Was the flag-pole on a prince's palace when
We looked at it through fingers crossed to riddle
In evening sunlight miracles for men.

It was the garden of the golden apples,
And when the Carrick train went by we knew
That we could never die till something happened
Like wishing for a fruit that never grew,

Or wanting to be up on Candle-Fort
Above the village with its shops and mill.
The racing cyclists' gasp-gapped reports
Hinted of pubs where life can drink his fill.

And when the sun went down into Drumcatton
And the New Moon by its little finger swung
From the telegraph wires, we knew how God had
    happened
And what the blackbird in the whitethorn sang.

It was the garden of the golden apples,
The half-way house where we had stopped a day
Before we took the west road to Drumcatton
Where the sun was always setting on the play.

The Great Hunger

[1]

Clay is the word and clay is the flesh
Where the potato-gatherers like mechanized scare-crows
    move
Along the side-fall of the hill – Maguire and his men.
If we watch them an hour is there anything we can
    prove
Of life as it is broken-backed over the Book
Of Death? Here crows gabble over worms and frogs
And the gulls like old newspapers are blown clear of the
    hedges, luckily.
Is there some light of imagination in these wet clods?
Or why do we stand here shivering?

                        Which of these men
Loved the light and the queen
Too long virgin? Yesterday was summer. Who was it
      promised marriage to himself
Before apples were hung from the ceilings for Hallowe'en?
We will wait and watch the tragedy to the last curtain
Till the last soul passively like a bag of wet clay
Rolls down the side of the hill, diverted by the angles
Where the plough missed or a spade stands, straitening
      the way.

A dog lying on a torn jacket under a heeled-up cart,
A horse nosing along the posied headland, trailing
A rusty plough. Three heads hanging between wide-
      apart
Legs. October playing a symphony on a slack wire paling.
Maguire watches the drills flattened out
And the flints that lit a candle for him on a June altar
Flameless. The drills slipped by and the days slipped by
And he trembled his head away and ran free from the
      world's halter,
And thought himself wiser than any man in the townland
When he laughed over pints of porter
Of how he came free from every net spread
In the gaps of experience. He shook a knowing head
And pretended to his soul
That children are tedious in hurrying fields of April
Where men are spanging across wide furrows.
Lost in the passion that never needs a wife –
The pricks that pricked were the pointed pins of harrows.
Children scream so loud that the crows could bring
The seed of an acre away with crow-rude jeers.
Patrick Maguire, he called his dog and he flung a stone in
      the air
And hallooed the birds away that were the birds of the years.

Turn over the weedy clods and tease out the tangled skeins.
What is he looking for there?
He thinks it is a potato, but we know better
Than his mud-gloved fingers probe in this insensitive hair.

'Move forward the basket and balance it steady
In this hollow. Pull down the shafts of that cart, Joe,
And straddle the horse,' Maguire calls.
'The wind's over Brannagan's, now that means rain.
Graip up some withered stalks and see that no potato falls
Over the tail-board going down the ruckety pass –
And *that's* a job we'll have to do in December,
Gravel it and build a kerb on the bog-side. Is that
        Cassidy's ass
Out in my clover? Curse o' God –
Where is that dog?
Never where he's wanted.' Maguire grunts and spits
Through a clay-wattled moustache and stares about him
        from the height.
His dream changes again like the cloud-swung wind
And he is not so sure now if his mother was right
When she praised the man who made a field his bride.

Watch him, watch him, that man on a hill whose spirit
Is a wet sack flapping about the knees of time.
He lives that his little fields may stay fertile when his
        own body
Is spread in the bottom of a ditch under two coulters
        crossed in Christ's Name.

He was suspicious in his youth as a rat near strange bread
When girls laughed; when they screamed he knew that
        meant
The cry of fillies in season. He could not walk
The easy road to his destiny. He dreamt
The innocence of young brambles to hooked treachery.

O the grip, O the grip of irregular fields! No man escapes.
It could not be that back of the hills love was free
And ditches straight.
No monster hand lifted up children and put down apes
As here.

                                'O God if I had been wiser!'
That was his sigh like the brown breeze in the thistles.
He looks towards his house and haggard. 'O God if I
    had been wiser!'
But now a crumpled leaf from the whitethorn bushes
Darts like a frightened robin, and the fence
Shows the green of after-grass through a little window,
And he knows that his own heart is calling his mother a liar.
God's truth is life – even the grotesque shapes of its
    foulest fire.

The horse lifts its head and crashes
Through the whins and stones
To lip late passion in the crawling clover.
In the gap there's a bush weighted with boulders like
    morality,
The fools of life bleed if they climb over.

The wind leans from Brady's, and the coltsfoot leaves
    are holed with rust,
Rain fills the cart-tracks and the sole-plate grooves;
A yellow sun reflects in Donaghmoyne
The poignant light in puddles shaped by hooves.

Come with me, Imagination, into this iron house
And we will watch from the doorway the years run
    back,
And we will know what a peasant's left hand wrote on
    the page.
Be easy, October. No cackle hen, horse neigh, tree sough,
    duck quack.

[II]

Maguire was faithful to death:
He stayed with his mother till she died
At the age of ninety-one.
She stayed too long,
Wife and mother in one.
When she died
The knuckle-bones were cutting the skin of her son's
        backside
And he was sixty-five.

O he loved his mother
Above all others,
O he loved his ploughs
And he loved his cows
And his happiest dream
Was to clean his arse
With perennial grass
On the bank of some summer stream;
To smoke his pipe
In a sheltered gripe
In the middle of July –
His face in a mist
And two stones in his fist
And an impotent worm on his thigh.

But his passion became a plague
For he grew feeble bringing the vague
Women of his mind to lust nearness,
Once a week at least flesh must make an appearance.

So Maguire got tired
Of the no-target gun fired
And returned to his headlands of carrots and cabbage

To the fields once again
Where eunuchs can be men
And life is more lousy than savage.

[III]

Poor Paddy Maguire, a fourteen-hour day
He worked for years. It was he that lit the fire
And boiled the kettle and gave the cows their hay.
His mother tall hard as a Protestant spire
Came down the stairs bare-foot at the kettle-call
And talked to her son sharply: 'Did you let
The hens out, you?' She had a venomous drawl
And a wizened face like moth-eaten leatherette.
Two black cats peeped between the banisters
And gloated over the bacon-fizzling pan.
Outside the window showed tin canisters.
The snipe of Dawn fell like a whirring noise
And Patrick on a headland stood alone.

The pull is on the traces, it is March
And a cold old black wind is blowing from Dundalk.
The twisting sod rolls over on her back –
The virgin screams before the irresistible sock.
No worry on Maguire's mind this day
Except that he forgot to bring his matches.
'Hop back there Polly, hoy back, woa, wae,'
From every second hill a neighbour watches
With all the sharpened interest of rivalry.
Yet sometimes when the sun comes through a gap
These men know God the Father in a tree:
The Holy Spirit is the rising sap,
And Christ will be the green leaves that will come
At Easter from the sealed and guarded tomb.

Primroses and the unearthly start of ferns
Among the blackthorn shadows in the ditch,
A dead sparrow and an old waistcoat. Maguire learns
As the horses turn slowly round the which is which
Of love and fear and things half born to mind.
He stands between the plough-handles and he sees
At the end of a long furrow his name signed
Among the poets, prostitute's. With all miseries
He is one. Here with the unfortunate
Who for half moments of paradise
Pay out good days and wait and wait
For sunlight-woven cloaks. O to be wise
As Respectability that knows the price of all things
And marks God's truth in pounds and pence and
    farthings.

[IV]

April, and no one able to calculate
How far is it to harvest. They put down
The seeds blindly with sensuous groping fingers,
And sensual sleep dreams subtly underground.
Tomorrow is Wednesday – who cares?
'Remember Eileen Farrelly? I was thinking
A man might do a damned sight worse . . .' That voice
    is blown
Through a hole in a garden wall –
And who was Eileen now cannot be known.

The cattle are out on grass,
The corn is coming up evenly.
The farm folk are hurrying to catch Mass:
Christ will meet them at the end of the world, the slow
    and speedier.
But the fields say: only Time can bless.

Maguire knelt beside a pillar where he could spit
Without being seen. He turned an old prayer round:
'Jesus, Mary and Joseph pray for us
Now and at the Hour.' Heaven dazzled death.
'Wonder should I cross-plough that turnip-ground.'
The tension broke. The congregation lifted its head
As one man and coughed in unison.
Five hundred hearts were hungry for life –
Who lives in Christ shall never die the death.
And the candle-lit Altar and the flowers
And the pregnant Tabernacle lifted a moment to
      Prophecy
Out of the clayey hours.
Maguire sprinkled his face with holy water
As the congregation stood up for the Last Gospel.
He rubbed the dust off his knees with his palm, and then
Coughed the prayer phlegm up from his throat and
      sighed: Amen.

Once one day in June when he was walking
Among his cattle in the Yellow Meadow
He met a girl carrying a basket –
And he was then a young and heated fellow.
Too earnest, too earnest! He rushed beyond the thing
To the unreal. And he saw Sin
Written in letters larger than John Bunyan dreamt of.
For the strangled impulse there is no redemption.
And that girl was gone and he was counting
The dangers in the fields where love ranted.
He was helpless. He saw his cattle
And stroked their flanks in lieu of wife to handle.
He would have changed the circle if he could,
The circle that was the grass track where he ran.
Twenty times a day he ran round the field
And still there was no winning post where the runner is
      cheered home.

Desperately he broke the tune,
But however he tried always the same melody crept up
    from the background,
The dragging step of a ploughman going home through
    the guttery
Headlands under an April-watery moon.
Religion, the fields and the fear of the Lord
And Ignorance giving him the coward's blow
He dare not rise to pluck the fantasies
From the fruited Tree of Life. He bowed his head
And saw a wet weed twined about his toe.

[V]

Evening at the cross-roads –
Heavy heads nodding out words as wise
As the rumination of cows after milking.
From the ragged road surface a boy picks up
A piece of gravel and stares at it – and then
He flings it across the elm tree on to the railway.
It means nothing,
Not a damn thing.
Somebody is coming over the metal railway bridge
And his hobnailed boots on the arches sound like a gong
Calling men awake. But the bridge is too narrow –
The men lift their heads a moment. That was only John,
So they dream on.

Night in the elms, night in the grass.
O we are too tired to go home yet. Two cyclists pass
Talking loudly of Kitty and Molly –
Horses or women? wisdom or folly?

A door closes on an evicted dog
Where prayers begin in Barney Meegan's kitchen;
Rosie curses the cat between her devotions;

The daughter prays that she may have three wishes –
Health and wealth and love –
From the fairy who is faith or hope or compounds of.

At the cross-roads the crowd had thinned out:
Last words are uttered. There is no tomorrow;
No future but only time stretched for the mowing of the
    hay
Or putting an axle in the turf-barrow.

Patrick Maguire went home and made cocoa
And broke a chunk off the loaf of wheaten bread;
His mother called down to him to look again
And make sure that the hen-house was locked. His sister
    grunted in bed,
The sound of a sow taking up a new position.
Pat opened his trousers wide over the ashes
And dreamt himself to lewd sleepiness.
The clock ticked on. Time passes.

[VI]

Health and wealth and love he too dreamed of in May
As he sat on the railway slope and watched the children
    of the place
Picking up a primrose here and a daisy there –
They were picking up life's truth singly. But he dreamt
    of the Absolute envased bouquet –
All or nothing. And it was nothing. For God is not all
In one place, complete and labelled like a case in a
    railway store
Till Hope comes in and takes it on his shoulder –
O Christ, that is what you have done for us:
In a crumb of bread the whole mystery is.

He read the symbol too sharply and turned
From the five simple doors of sense
To the door whose combination lock has puzzled
Philosopher and priest and common dunce.

Men build their heavens as they build their circles
Of friends. God is in the bits and pieces of Everyday –
A kiss here and a laugh again, and sometimes tears,
A pearl necklace round the neck of poverty.

He sat on the railway slope and watched the evening,
Too beautifully perfect to use,
And his three wishes were three stones too sharp to sit
   on,
Too hard to carve. Three frozen idols of a speechless
   muse.

[VII]

'Now go to Mass and pray and confess your sins
And you'll have all the luck,' his mother said.
He listened to the lie that is a woman's screen
Around a conscience when soft thighs are spread.
And all the while she was setting up the lie
She trusted in Nature that never deceives.
But her son took it as the literal truth.
Religion's walls expand to the push of nature. Morality
   yields
To sense – but not in little tillage fields.

Life went on like that. One summer morning
Again through a hay-field on her way to the shop –
The grass was wet and over-leaned the path –
And Agnes held her skirts sensationally up,
And not because the grass was wet either.
A man was watching her, Patrick Maguire.

She was in love with passion and its weakness
And the wet grass could never cool the fire
That radiated from her unwanted womb
In that country, in that metaphysical land
Where flesh was a thought more spiritual than music
Among the stars – out of the reach of the peasant's
         hand.

Ah, but the priest was one of the people too –
A farmer's son – and surely he knew
The needs of a brother and sister.
Religion could not be a counter-irritant like a blister,
But the certain standard measured and known
By which a man might re-make his soul though all walls
         were down
And all earth's pedestalled gods thrown.

[VIII]

Sitting on a wooden gate,
Sitting on a wooden gate,
Sitting on a wooden gate
He didn't care a damn.
Said whatever came into his head,
Said whatever came into his head,
Said whatever came into his head
And inconsequently sang.
Inconsequently sang
While his world withered away,
He had a cigarette to smoke and a pound to spend
On drink the next Saturday.
His cattle were fat
And his horses all that
Midsummer grass could make them.
The young women ran wild
And dreamed of a child.

Joy dreams though the fathers might forsake them
But no one would take them,
No one would take them;
No man could ever see
That their skirts had loosed buttons,
Deliberately loosed buttons.
O the men were as blind as could be.
And Patrick Maguire
From his purgatory fire
Called the gods of the Christian to prove
That this twisted skein
Was the necessary pain
And not the rope that was strangling true love.

But sitting on a wooden gate
Sometime in July
When he was thirty-four or five
He gloried in the lie:
He made it read the way it should,
He made life read the evil good
While he cursed the ascetic brotherhood
Without knowing why.
Sitting on a wooden gate
All, all alone
He sang and laughed
Like a man quite daft,
Or like a man on a channel raft
He fantasied forth his groan.
Sitting on a wooden gate,
Sitting on a wooden gate,
Sitting on a wooden gate
He rode in day-dream cars.
He locked his body with his knees
When the gate swung too much in the breeze.
But while he caught high ecstasies
Life slipped between the bars.

[IX]

He gave himself another year,
Something was bound to happen before then –
The circle would break down
And he would curve the new one to his own will.
A new rhythm is a new life
And in it marriage is hung and money.
He would be a new man walking through unbroken
    meadows
Of dawn in the year of One.

The poor peasant talking to himself in a stable door –
An ignorant peasant deep in dung.
What can the passers-by think otherwise?
Where is his silver bowl of knowledge hung?
Why should men be asked to believe in a soul
That is only the mark of a hoof in guttery gaps?
A man is what is written on the label.
And the passing world stares but no one stops
To look closer. So back to the growing crops
And the ridges he never loved.
Nobody will ever know how much tortured poetry the
    pulled weeds on the ridge wrote
Before they withered in the July sun,
Nobody will ever read the wild, sprawling, scrawling
    mad woman's signature,
The hysteria and the boredom of the enclosed nun of his
    thought.
Like the afterbirth of a cow stretched on a branch in the
    wind
Life dried in the veins of these women and men:
The grey and grief and unlove,
The bones in the backs of their hands,
And the chapel pressing its low ceiling over them.

Sometimes they did laugh and see the sunlight,
A narrow slice of divine instruction.
Going along the river at the bend of Sunday
The trout played in the pools encouragement
To jump in love though death bait the hook.
And there would be girls sitting on the grass banks of
     lanes
Stretch-legged and lingering staring –
A man might take one of them if he had the courage.
But 'No' was in every sentence of their story
Except when the public-house came in and shouted its
     piece.

The yellow buttercups and the bluebells among the
     whin bushes
On rocks in the middle of ploughing
Was a bright spoke in the wheel
Of the peasant's mill.
The goldfinches on the railway paling were worth
     looking at –
A man might imagine then
Himself in Brazil and these birds the Birds of Paradise
And the Amazon and the romance traced on the school
     map lived again.

Talk in evening corners and under trees
Was like an old book found in a king's tomb.
The children gathered round like students and listened
And some of the saga defied the draught in the open
     tomb
And was not blown.

[X]

Their intellectual life consisted in reading
Reynolds' News or the *Sunday Dispatch*
With sometimes an old almanac brought down from the
    ceiling
Or a school reader brown with the droppings of thatch.
The sporting results or the headlines or war
Was a humbug profound as the highbrow's Arcana.
Pat tried to be wise to the abstraction of all that
But its secret dribbled down his waistcoat like a drink
    from a strainer.
He wagered a bob each way on the Derby,
He got a straight tip from a man in a shop –
A double from the Guineas it was and thought himself
A master mathematician when one of them came up
And he could explain how much he'd have drawn
On the double if the second leg had followed the first.
He was betting on form and breeding, he claimed,
And the man that did that could never be burst.
After that they went on to the war, and the generals
On both sides were shown to be stupid as hell.
If he'd taken *that* road, they remarked of a Marshal,
He'd have . . . O they know their geography well.
This was their university. Maguire was an
    undergraduate
Who dreamed from his lowly position of rising
To a professorship like Larry McKenna or Duffy
Or the pig-gelder Nallon whose knowledge was amazing.
'A treble, full multiple odds . . . That's flat porter . . .
My turnips are destroyed with the blackguardly crows . . .
Another one . . . No, you're wrong about that thing I
    was telling you . . .
Did you part with your filly, Jack? I heard that you sold her . . .
The students were all savants by the time of pub-close.

[XI]

A year passed and another hurried after it
And Patrick Maguire was still six months behind life –
His mother six months ahead of it;
His sister straddle-legged across it: –
One leg in hell and the other in heaven
And between the purgatory of middle-aged virginity –
She prayed for release to heaven or hell.
His mother's voice grew thinner like a rust-worn knife
But it cut more venomously as it thinned,
It cut him up the middle till he became more woman
        than man,
And it cut through to his mind before the end.

Another field whitened in the April air
And the harrows rattled over the seed.
He gathered the loose stones off the ridges carefully
And grumbled to his men to hurry. He looked like a
        man who could give advice
To foolish young fellows. He was forty-seven,
And there was depth in his jaw and his voice was the
        voice of a great cattle-dealer,
A man with whom the fair-green gods break even.
'I think I ploughed that lea the proper depth,
She ought to give a crop if any land gives . . .
Drive slower with the foal-mare, Joe.'
Joe, a young man of imagined wives,
Smiled to himself and answered like a slave:
'You needn't fear or fret.
I'm taking her as easy, as easy as . . .
Easy there Fanny, easy pet.'

They loaded the day-scoured implements on the cart
As the shadows of poplars crookened the furrows.

It was the evening, evening. Patrick was forgetting to be
    lonely
As he used to be in Aprils long ago.
It was the menopause, the misery-pause.

The schoolgirls passed his house laughing every morning
And sometimes they spoke to him familiarly –
He had an idea. Schoolgirls of thirteen
Would see no political intrigue in an old man's friendship.
Love
The heifer waiting to be nosed by the old bull.
That notion passed too – there was the danger of talk
And jails are narrower than the five-sod ridge
And colder than the black hills facing Armagh in February.
He sinned over the warm ashes again and his crime
The law's long arm could not serve with 'time'.

His face set like an old judge's pose:
Respectability and righteousness,
Stand for no nonsense.
The priest from the altar called Patrick Maguire's name
To hold the collecting box in the chapel door
During all the Sundays of May.
His neighbours envied him his holy rise,
But he walked down from the church with affected
    indifference
And took the measure of heaven angle-wise.

He still could laugh and sing,
But not the wild laugh or the abandoned harmony now
That called the world to new silliness from the top of a
    wooden gate
When thirty-five could take the sparrow's bow.
Let us be kind, let us be kind and sympathetic:
Maybe life is not for joking or for finding happiness in –
This tiny light in Oriental Darkness
Looking out chance windows of poetry or prayer.

And the grief and defeat of men like these peasants
Is God's way – maybe – and we must not want too much
To see.
The twisted thread is stronger than the wind-swept fleece.
And in the end who shall rest in truth's high peace?
Or whose is the world now, even now?
O let us kneel where the blind ploughman kneels
And learn to live without despairing
In a mud-walled space –
Illiterate, unknown and unknowing.
Let us kneel where he kneels
And feel what he feels.

One day he saw a daisy and he thought it
Reminded him of his childhood –
He stopped his cart to look at it.
Was there a fairy hiding behind it?

He helped a poor woman whose cow
Had died on her;
He dragged home a drunken man on a winter's night;
And one rare moment he heard the young people playing
        on the railway stile
And he wished them happiness and whatever they most
        desired from life.

He saw the sunlight and begrudged no man
His share of what the miserly soil and soul
Gives in a season to a ploughman.
And he cried for his own loss one late night on the pillow
And yet thanked the God who had arranged these things.

Was he then a saint?
A Mat Talbot of Monaghan?

His sister Mary Anne spat poison at the children
Who sometimes came to the door selling raffle tickets
For holy funds.

'Get out you little tramps!' she would scream
As she shook to the hens an apronful of crumbs,
But Patrick often put his hand deep down
In his trouser-pocket and fingered out a penny
Or maybe a tobacco-stained caramel.
'You're soft,' said the sister; 'with other people's money
It's not a bit funny.'

The cards are shuffled and the deck
Laid flat for cutting – Tom Malone
Cut for trump. I think we'll make
This game, the last, a tanner one.
Hearts. Right. I see you're breaking
Your two-year-old. Play quick, Maguire,
The clock there says it['s] half-past ten –
Kate, throw another sod on that fire.
One of the card-players laughs and spits
Into the flame across a shoulder.
Outside, a noise like a rat
Among the hen-roosts. The cock crows over
The frosted townland of the night.
Eleven o'clock and still the game
Goes on and the players seem to be
Drunk in an Orient opium den.
Midnight, one o'clock, two.
Somebody's leg has fallen asleep.
What about home? Maguire are you
Using your double-tree this week?
Why? do you want it? Play the ace.
There's it, and that's the last card for me.
A wonderful night, we had. Duffy's place
Is very convenient. Is that a ghost or a tree?
And so they go home with dragging feet
And their voices rumble like laden carts.
And they are happy as the dead or sleeping . . .
I should have led that ace of hearts.

[XII]

The fields were bleached white,
The wooden tubs full of water
Were white in the winds
That blew through Brannagan's Gap on their way from
     Siberia;
The cows on the grassless heights
Followed the hay that had wings –
The February fodder that hung itself on the black branches
Of the hilltop hedge.
A man stood beside a potato-pit
And clapped his arms
And pranced on the crisp roots
And shouted to warm himself.
Then he buck-leaped about the potatoes
And scooped them into a basket.
He looked like a bucking suck-calf
Whose spine was being tickled.
Sometimes he stared across the bogs
And sometimes he straightened his back and vaguely
     whistled
A tune that weakened his spirit
And saddened his terrier dog's.
A neighbour passed with a spade on his shoulder
And Patrick Maguire bent like a bridge
Whistled – good morning under his oxter,
And the man the other side of the hedge
Champed his spade on the road at his toes
And talked an old sentimentality
While the wind blew under his clothes.

The mother sickened and stayed in bed all day,
Her head hardly dented the pillow, so light and thin it
     had worn,
But she still enquired after the household affairs.
She held the strings of her children's Punch and Judy
     and when a mouth opened
It was her truth that the dolls would have spoken
If they hadn't been made of wood and tin –
'Did you open the barn door, Pat, to let the young
     calves in?'
The priest called to see her every Saturday
And she told him her troubles and fears:
'If Mary Anne was settled I'd die in peace –
I'm getting on in years.'
'You were a good woman,' said the priest,
'And your children will miss you when you're gone.
The likes of you this parish never knew,
I'm sure they'll not forget the work you've done.'
She reached five bony crooks under the tick –
'Five pounds for Masses – won't you say them quick.'
She died one morning in the beginning of May
And a shower of sparrow-notes was the litany for her
     dying.
The holy water was sprinkled on the bed-clothes
And her children stood around the bed and cried because
     it was too late for crying.
A mother dead! The tired sentiment:
'Mother mother' was a shallow pool
Where sorrow hardly could wash its feet . . .
Mary Anne came away from the deathbed and boiled
     the calves their gruel.
O what was I doing when the procession passed?
Where was I looking?
Young women and men
And I might have joined them.

Who bent the coin of my destiny
That it stuck in the slot?
I remember a night we walked
Through the moon of Donaghmoyne,
Four of us seeking adventure –
It was midsummer forty years ago.
Now I know
The moment that gave the turn to my life.
O Christ! I am locked in a stable with pigs and cows for ever.

[XIII]

The world looks on
And talks of the peasant:
The peasant has no worries;
In his little lyrical fields
He ploughs and sows;
He eats fresh food,
He loves fresh women,
He is his own master
As it was in the Beginning
The simpleness of peasant life.
The birds that sing for him are eternal choirs,
Everywhere he walks there are flowers.
His heart is pure,
His mind is clear,
He can talk to God as Moses and Isaiah talked –
The peasant who is only one remove from the beasts he drives.
The travellers stop their cars to gape over the green
      bank into his fields: –

There is the source from which all cultures rise,
And all religions,
There is the pool in which the poet dips
And the musician.

Without the peasant base civilization must die,
Unless the clay is in the mouth the singer's singing is
    useless.
The travellers touch the roots of the grass and feel
    renewed
When they grasp the steering wheels again.
The peasant is the unspoiled child of Prophecy,
The peasant is all virtues – let us salute him without irony
The peasant ploughman who is half a vegetable –
Who can react to sun and rain and sometimes even
Regret that the Maker of Light had not touched him
    more intensely.
Brought him up from the sub-soil to an existence
Of conscious joy. He was not born blind.
He is not always blind: Sometimes the cataract yields
To sudden stone-falling or the desire to breed.

The girls pass along the roads
And he can remember what man is,
But there is nothing he can do.
Is there nothing he can do?
Is there no escape?
No escape, no escape.

The cows and horses breed,
And the potato-seed
Gives a bud and a root and rots
In the good mother's way with her sons;
The fledged bird is thrown
From the nest – on its own.
But the peasant in his little acres is tied
To a mother's womb by the wind-toughened navel-cord
Like a goat tethered to the stump of a tree –
He circles around and around wondering why it should be.
No crash,
No drama.

That was how his life happened.
No mad hooves galloping in the sky,
But the weak, washy way of true tragedy –
A sick horse nosing around the meadow for a clean
    place to die.

[XIV]

We may come out into the October reality, Imagination,
The sleety wind no longer slants to the black hill where
    Maguire
And his men are now collecting the scattered harness
    and baskets.
The dog sitting on a wisp of dry stalks
Watches them through the shadows.
'Back in, back in.' One talks to the horse as to a brother.
Maguire himself is patting a potato-pit against the weather –
An old man fondling a new-piled grave:
'Joe, I hope you didn't forget to hide the spade
For there's rogues in the townland. Hide it flat in a furrow.
I think we ought to be finished by tomorrow.'
Their voices through the darkness sound like voices from
    a cave,
A dull thudding far away, futile, feeble, far away,
First cousins to the ghosts of the townland.

A light stands in a window. Mary Anne
Has the table set and the tea-pot waiting in the ashes.
She goes to the door and listens and then she calls
From the top of the haggard-wall:
'What's keeping you
And the cows to be milked and all the other work
    there's to do?'
'All right, all right
We'll not stay here all night.'

Applause, applause,
The curtain falls.
Applause, applause
From the homing carts and the trees
And the bawling cows at the gates.
From the screeching water-hens
And the mill-race heavy with the Lammas floods curving
  over the weir.
A train at the station blowing off steam
And the hysterical laughter of the defeated everywhere.
Night, and the futile cards are shuffled again.
Maguire spreads his legs over the impotent cinders that
  wake no manhood now
And he hardly looks to see which card is trump.
His sister tightens her legs and her lips and frizzles up
Like the wick of an oil-less lamp.
The curtain falls –
Applause, applause.

Maguire is not afraid of death, the Church will light
  him a candle
To see his way through the vaults and he'll understand
  the
Quality of the clay that dribbles over his coffin.
He'll know the names of the roots that climb down to
  tickle his feet.
And he will feel no different than when he walked
  through Donaghmoyne.
If he stretches out a hand – a wet clod,
If he opens his nostrils – a dungy smell;
If he opens his eyes once in a million years –
Through a crack in the crust of the earth he may see a
  face nodding in
Or a woman's legs. Shut them again for that sight is sin.

He will hardly remember that life happened to him —
Something was brighter a moment. Somebody sang in
 the distance.
A procession passed down a mesmerized street.
He remembers names like Easter and Christmas
By the colour his fields were.
Maybe he will be born again, a bird of an angel's
 conceit
To sing the gospel of life
To a music as flightily tangent
As a tune on an oboe.
And the serious look of the fields will have changed to
 the leer of a hobo
Swaggering celestially home to his three wishes granted.
Will that be? will that be?
Or is the earth right that laughs: haw haw
And does not believe
In an unearthy law.
The earth that says:
Patrick Maguire, the old peasant, can neither be damned
 nor glorified:
The graveyard in which he will lie will be just a deep-
 drilled potato-field
Where the seed gets no chance to come through
To the fun of the sun.
The tongue in his mouth is the root of a yew.
Silence, silence. The story is done.

He stands in the doorway of his house
A ragged sculpture of the wind,
October creaks the rotted mattress,
The bedposts fall. No hope. No. No lust.
The hungry fiend
Screams the apocalypse of clay
In every corner of this land.

Lough Derg

From Cavan and from Leitrim and from Mayo,
From all the thin-faced parishes where hills
Are perished noses running peaty water,
They come to Lough Derg to fast and pray and beg
With all the bitterness of nonentities, and the envy
Of the inarticulate when dealing with an artist.
Their hands push closed the doors that God holds
    open.
Love-sunlit is an enchanter in June's hours
And flowers and light. These to shopkeepers and small
    lawyers
Are heresies up beauty's sleeve.

The naïve and simple go on pilgrimage too,
Lovers trying to take God's truth for granted . . .
Listen to the chanted
Evening devotions in the limestone church,
For this is Lough Derg, St Patrick's Purgatory.
He came to this island-acre of greenstone once
To be shut of the smug too-faithful. The story
Is different now.
Solicitors praying for cushy jobs
To be County Registrar or Coroner,
Shopkeepers threatened with sharper rivals
Than any hook-nosed foreigner.
Mothers whose daughters are Final Medicals,
Too heavy-hipped for thinking,
Wives whose husbands have angina pectoris,
Wives whose husbands have taken to drinking.

But there were the sincere as well,
The innocent who feared the hell

45

Of sin. The girl who had won
A lover and the girl who had none
Were both in trouble
Trying to encave in the rubble
Of these rocks the Real,
The part that can feel.
And the half-pilgrims too,
They who are the true
Spirit of Ireland, who joke
Through the Death-mask and take
Virgins of heaven or flesh,
Were on Lough Derg Island
Wanting some half-wish.

Over the black waves of the lake trip the last echoes
Of the bell that has shooed through the chapel door
The last pilgrims, like hens to roost.
The sun through Fermanagh's furze fingers
Looks now on the deserted penance rings of stone
Where only John Flood on St Kevin's Bed lingers
With the sexton's heaven-sure stance, the man who
       knows
The ins and outs of religion . . .
'Hail glorious St Patrick' a girl sings above
The old-man drone of the harmonium.
The rosary is said and Benediction.
The Sacramental sun turns round and 'Holy, Holy,
       Holy'
The pilgrims cry, striking their breasts in Purgatory.

The same routine and ritual now
As serves for street processions or Congresses

That take all shapes of souls as a living theme
In a novel refuses nothing. No truth oppresses.

Women and men in bare feet turn again
To the iron crosses and the rutted Beds,
Their feet are swollen and their bellies empty –
But something that is Ireland's secret leads
These petty mean people
For here's the day of a poor soul freed
To a marvellous beauty above its head.
The Castleblaney grocer trapped in the moment's need
Puts out a hand and writes what he cannot read,
A wisdom astonished at every turn
By some angel that writes in the oddest words.
When he will walk again in Muckno Street
He'll hear from the kitchens of fair-day eating houses
In the after-bargain carouses
News from a country beyond the range of birds.

The lake waves caught the concrete stilts of the Basilica
That spread like a bulldog's hind paws. A Leitrim man,
With a face as sad as a flooded hay-field,
Leaned in an angle of the walls with his rosary beads in
        his hands.

Beside St Brigid's Cross – an ancient relic
A fragment of the Middle Ages set
Into the modern masonry of the conventional Basilica
Where everything is ordered and correct –
A queue of pilgrims waiting to renounce
The World, the Flesh, the Devil and all his house.

Like young police recruits being measured
Each pilgrim flattened backwards to the wall
And stretched his arms wide
As he cried:
'I renounce the World, the Flesh and the Devil';
Three times they cried out. A country curate
Stared with a curate leer – he was proud.
The booted
Prior passes by ignoring all the crowd.

'I renounce the World,' a young woman cried.
Her breasts stood high in the pagan sun.
'I renounce . . .' an old monk followed. Then a fat lawyer.
They rejected one by one
The music of Time's choir.

A half-pilgrim looked up at the Carrara marbles,
St Patrick wearing an alb with no stitch dropped.
Once he held a shamrock in his hand
But the stem was flawed and it got lost.

St Brigid and the Blessed Virgin flanked
Ireland's national apostle
On the south-west of the island on the gravel-path
Opposite the men's hostel.

Around the island like soldiers quartered round a
        barrack-yard
There were houses, and a stall where agnisties
And Catholic Truth pamphlets were sold,
And at the pier end, the grey chapel of St Mary's.

The middle of the island looked like the memory
Of some village evicted by the Famine,

Some corner of a field beside a well
Old stumps of walls where a stunted boortree is
     growing.
These were the holy cells of saintly men –
O that was the place where Mickey Fehan lived
And the Reillys before they went to America in the
     Fifties.
No, this is Lough Derg in County Donegal –
So much alike is our historical
And spiritual pattern, a heap
Of stones anywhere is consecrated
By love's terrible need.

On Lough Derg, too, the silver strands
Of the individual sometimes show
Through the fabric of prison anonymity.
One man's private trouble transcending the divinity
Of the prayer-locked multitude.
A vein of humanity that can bleed
Through the thickest hide.
And such a plot unfolds a moment, so –

In a crevice between the houses and the lake
A tall red-headed man of thirty slouches,
A half-pilgrim who hated prayer,
All truth for which St Patrick's Purgatory vouches.
He was a small farmer who was fond of literature
In a country-schoolmaster way.
He skimmed the sentiment of every pool of experience
And talked heresy lightly from distances
Where nothing was terrifyingly Today
Where he felt he could be safe and say or sin –
But Christ sometimes bleeds in the museum.

It was the first day of his pilgrimage.
He came to Lough Derg to please the superstition
Which says, 'At least the thing can do no harm'
Yet he alone went out with Jesus fishing.

An ex-monk from Dublin, a broad-faced man
With his Franciscan habit sweeping was a pilgrim
A sad priest staggering in a megrim
Between doubt and vanity's courtesan.
He had fallen once and secretly, no shame
Tainted the young girl's name,
A convent schoolgirl knowing
Nothing of earth sowing.
He took her three times
As in his day-dreams
These things happened.
Three times finds all
The notes of body's madrigal.
'Twas a failing otherwise
Lost him his priestly faculties.

Barefoot in the kitchen
Of John Flood's cottage
Where the girls of Donegal sat, laughing round on
    stools,
And iron cranes and crooks
Were loaded with black pots,
And holy-looking women kept going in and out of the
    rooms
As though some man was a-waking . . .
The red-haired man came in
And saw among the loud cold women one who
Was not a Holy Biddy
With a rat-trap on her diddy,

But something from the unconverted kingdom
The beauty that has turned
Convention into forests
Where Adam wanders deranged with half a memory;
And red-haired Robert Fitzsimons
Saw Aggie Meegan, and quietly
An angel was turning over the pages of
     Mankind's history.
He must have her, she was waiting
By the unprotected gable
Of asceticism's granite castle. The masonry's down
And the sun coming in is blood
The green of trees is lust
He saw from the unpeopled country into a town.

Let beauty bag or burst,
The sharp points of truth may not be versed
Too smoothly, but the truth must go in as it occurred,
A bulb of light in the shadows of Lough Derg.

The first evening they prayed till nine o'clock
Around the gravel rings, a hundred decades
Of rosaries until they hardly knew what words meant –
Their own names when they spoke them sounded
     mysterious.
They knelt and prayed and rose and prayed
And circled the crosses and kissed the stones
Never looking away from the brimstone bitterness
To the little islands of Pan held in the crooked elbow of
     the lake.
They closed their eyes to Donegal and the white houses
On the slope of the northern hills.

And these pilgrims of a western reason
Were not pursuing French-hot miracles.
There were hundreds of them tripping one another
Upon the pilgrim way (O God of Truth,
Keep him who tells this story straight,
Let no cheap insincerity shape his mouth).
These men and boys were not led there
By priests of Maynooth or stories of Italy or Spain
For this is the penance of the poor
Who know what beauty hides in misery
As beggars, fools and eastern fakirs know.

Black tea, dry bread.
Yesterday's pilgrims went upstairs to bed
And as they slept
The vigil in St Patrick's prison was kept
By the others. The Evening Star
Looked into Purgatory whimsically. Night dreams are
Simple and catching as music-hall tunes
Of the Nineties. We'll ramble through the brambles of
    starry-strange Junes.

On a seat beside the women's hostel four men
Sat and talked spare minutes away;
It was like Sunday evening on a country road
Light and gay.
The talk was 'There's a man
Who must be twenty stone weight – a horrid size . . .'
'Larry O'Duff . . . yes, like a balloon
Or a new tick of chaff . . . Lord, did anyone ever see
    clearer skies?'
'No rain a while yet, Joe,
And the turnips could be doing with a sup, you know.'

And in the women's talk too, was woven
Such earth to cool the burning brain of Heaven.
On the steps of the church the monks talked
To Robert of art, music, literature.
'Genius is not measured,' he said,
'In prudent feet and inches
Old Justice burns the work of Raphael –
Justice was God until he saw His Son
Falling in love with earth's fantastic one,
The woman in whose dunghill of emotion
Grows flowers of poetry, music, and the old
Kink in the mind, the fascination
Of sin troubled the mind of God
Until He thought of Charity . . .
Have you known Charity? Have I?'
Aggie Meegan passed by
To vigil. Robert was puzzled, Where
Grew the germ of this crooked prayer?
The girl was thrilling as joy's despair.

A schoolmaster from Roscommon led
The vigil prayers that night.
'Hail Queen of Heaven' they sang at twelve.
Someone snored near the porch. A bright
Moon sailed in from the County Tyrone
By the water route that he might make
Queer faces in the stained-glassed windows. Why should
     sun
Have all the fun?
'Our vows of Baptism we again take . . .'
Every Rosary brought the morning nearer.
The schoolmaster looked at his watch and said:
'Out now for a mouthful of fresh air –
A ten-minute break to clear the head.'

It was cold in the rocky draughts between the houses.
Old women tried
To pull bare feet close to their bellies.
Three o'clock rang from the Prior's house clock.
In the hostels pilgrims slept away a three-day fast.

On the cell-wall beside the sycamore tree,
The tree that never knew a bird,
Aggie sat fiddling with her Rosary
And doubting the power of Lough Derg
To save the season's rose of life
With the ponderous fingers of prayer's philosophy.

Robert was a philosopher, a false one
Who ever takes a sledge to swat a fly.
He talked to the girls as a pedant professor
Talking in a university.
The delicate precise immediacy
That sees a flower half a foot away
He could not learn. He spoke to Aggie
Of powers, passions, with the *naïveté*
Of a ploughman. She did not understand –
She only knew that she could hold his hand
If he stood closer. 'Virtue is sublime,'
He said, 'and it is virtue is the frame
Of all love and learning . . .'
'I want to tell you something,' she whispered,
'Because you are different and will know . . .'
'You don't need to tell me anything, you could not,
For your innocence is pure glass that I see through.'
'You'd be surprised,' she smiled. O God, he
    gasped
To his soul, what could she mean by that?

They watched the lake waves clapping cold hands
    together
And saw the morning breaking as it breaks
Over a field where a man is watching a calving cow.
New life, new day.
A half-pilgrim saw it as a rabbiter
Poaching in wood sees
Primeval magic among the trees.

The rusty cross of St Patrick had a dozen
Devotees clustered around it at four o'clock.
Bare knees were going round St Brendan's Bed.
A boy was standing like a ballet dancer poised on the
    rock
Under the belfry; he stared over at Donegal
Where the white houses on the side of the hills
Popped up like mushrooms in September.
The sun was smiling on a thousand hayfields
That hour, and he must have thought Lough Derg
More unreasonable than ordinary stone.
Perhaps it was an iceberg
That he had glanced at on his journey from Japan,
But the iceberg filled a glass of water
And poured it to the honour of the sun.
Lough Derg in the dawn poured rarer cups. Prayer
And fast that makes the sourest drink rare.
Was that St Paul
Riding his ass down a lane in Donegal?
Christ was lately dead,
Men were afraid
With a new fear, the fear
Of love. There was a laugh freed
For ever and for ever. The Apostles' Creed

Was a fireside poem, the talk of the town . . .
They remember a man who has seen Christ in his thorny
    crown.

John Flood came out and climbed the rock to ring
His bell for six o'clock. He spoke to the pilgrims:
'Was the night fine?'
'Wonderful, wonderful,' they answered, 'not too cold –
Thank God we have the worst part over us.'

The bell brought the sleepers from their cubicles.
Grey-faced boatmen were getting out a boat.
Mass was said. Another day began.
The penance wheel turned round again.
Pilgrims went out in boats, singing
'O Fare Thee Well, Lough Derg' as they waved
Affection to the persecuting stones.

The Prior went with them – suavely, goodily
Priestly, painfully directing the boats.
They who were left behind
Felt like the wellwishers who keep house when the
    funeral
Has left for the chapel.

Lough Derg overwhelmed the individual imagination
And the personal tragedy.
Only God thinks of the dying sparrow
In the middle of a war.

The ex-monk, farmer and the girl
Melted in the crowd
Where only God, the poet
Followed with interest till he found

Their secret, and constructed from
The chaos of its fire
A reasonable document.

A man's the centre of the world,
A man is not an anonymous
Member of the general public.
The Communion of Saints
Is a Communion of individuals.
God the Father is the Father
Of each one of us.

Then there was war, the slang, the contemporary
        touch,
The ideologies of the daily papers.
They must seem realer, Churchill, Stalin, Hitler,
Than ideas in the contemplative cloister.
The battles where ten thousand men die
Are more significant than a peasant's emotional problem.
But wars will be merely dry bones in histories
And these common people real living creatures in it
On the unwritten spaces between the lines.
A man throws himself prostrate
And God lies down beside him like a woman
Consoling the hysteria of her lover
That sighs his passion emptily:
'The next time, love, you shall faint in me.'

'Don't ask for life,' the monk said.
'If you meet her
Be easy with your affection;
She's a traitor
To those who love too much
As I have done.'

'What have you done?' said Robert
'That you've come
To St Patrick's Purgatory?'
The monk told his story
Of how he thought that he
Could make reality
Of the romance of the books
That told of Popes,
Men of genius who drew
Wild colours on the flat page. He knew
Now that madness is not knowing
That laws for the mown hay
Will not serve that which is growing.
Through Lough Derg's fast and meditation
He learned the wisdom of his generation.
He was satisfied now his heart
Was free from the coquetry of art.

Something was unknown
To Robert, not long,
For Aggie told him all
That hour as they sat on the wall
Of Brendan's cell:
Birth, bastardy and murder –
He only heard rocks crashing distantly
When John Flood rang the midday bell.

Now the three of them got out of the story altogether
Almost. Now they were not three egotists
But part of the flood of humanity,
Anonymous, never to write or be written.
They vanish among the forests and we see them
Appearing among the trees for seconds.
Lough Derg rolls its caravan before us
And as the pilgrims pass their thoughts are reckoned.

St Patrick was there, that peasant-faced man,
Whose image was embroidered on political banners
In the days of the AOH and John Redmond.
A kindly soft man this Patrick was, like a farmer
To whom no man might be afraid to tell a story
Of bawdy life as it goes in country places.
Was St Patrick like that?
A shamrock in a politician's hat
Yesterday. Today
The sentimentality of an Urban Councillor
Moving an address of welcome to the Cardinal.
All Ireland's Patricks were present on Lough Derg,
All Ireland that froze for want of Europe.

'And who are you?' said the poet speaking to
The old Leitrim man.
He said, 'I can tell you
What I am.
Servant girls bred my servility:
When I stoop
It is my mother's mother['s] mother's mother
Each one in turn being called in to spread –
"Wider with your legs," the master of the house said.
Domestic servants taken back and front.
That's why I'm servile. It is not the poverty
Of soil in Leitrim that makes me raise my hat
To fools with fifty pounds in a paper bank.
Domestic servants, no one has told
Their generations as it is, as I
Show the cowardice of the man whose mothers were
        whored
By five generations of capitalist and lord.'

Time passed.
Three boatloads of Dublin's unemployed came in
At three o'clock led by a priest from Thomas Street
To glutton over the peat-filtered water
And sit back drunk when jobs are found
In the Eternal factory where the boss
Himself must punch the clock.

And the day crawled lazily
Along the orbit of Purgatory.

A baker from Rathfriarland
A solicitor from Derry
A parish priest from Wicklow
A civil servant from Kerry
Sat on the patch of grass,
Their stations for the day
Completed – all things arranged,
Nothing in doubt, nothing gone astray.
O the boredom of Purgatory
Said the poet then,
This piety that hangs like a fool's, unthought,
This certainty in men,
This three days too-goodness,
Too-neighbourly cries
Temptation to murder
Mediocrities.

The confession boxes in St Mary's chapel hum
And it is evening now. Prose prayers become
Odes and sonnets.
There is a shrine with money heaped upon it
Before Our Lady of Miraculous Succour.

A woman said her litany:
That my husband may get his health

We beseech thee hear us
That my son Joseph may pass the Intermediate
　　We beseech thee hear us
That my daughter Eileen may do well at her music
　　We beseech thee hear us
That her aunt may remember us in her will
　　We beseech thee hear us
That there may be good weather for the hay
　　We beseech thee hear us
That my indigestion may be cured
　　We beseech thee hear us
O Mother of Perpetual Succour! in temptation
　　Be you near us.
And some deep prayers were shaped like sonnets –

O good St Anthony, your poor client asks
That he may have one moment in his arms
The girl I am thinking of this minute –
I'd love her even if she had no farms
Or a four-footed beast in a stable;
Her father is old, doting down the lanes,
There isn't anyone as able
As I am for cocking hay or cleaning drains.
All this that I am is an engine running
Light down the narrow-gauge railway of life.
St Anthony, I ask for Mary Gunning
Of Rathdrumskean to be my wife.
My strength is a skull battering the wall
Where a remand-prisoner is losing his soul.

St Anne, I am a young girl from Castleblaney,
One of a farmer's six grown daughters.
Our little farm, when the season's rainy,
Is putty spread on stones. The surface waters
Soak all the fields of this north-looking townland.

Last year we lost our acre of potatoes
And my mother with unmarried daughters round her
Is soaked like our soil in savage natures.
She tries to be as kind as any mother
But what can a mother be in such a house
With arguments going on and such a bother
About the half-boiled pots and unmilked cows.
O Patron of the pure woman who lacks a man,
Let me be free I beg of you, St Anne.

O Sacred Heart of Jesus, I ask of you
A job so I can settle down and marry;
I want to live a decent life. And through
The flames of St Patrick's Purgatory
I go offering every stone-bruise, all my hunger;
In the back-room of my penance I am weaving
An inside-shirt for charity. How longer
Must a fifty-shilling-a-week job be day-dreaming?
The dole and empty minds and empty pockets,
Cup Finals seen from the branches of a tree,
Old films that break the eye-balls in their sockets,
A toss-pit. This is life for such as me.
And I know a girl and I know a room to be let
And a job in a builder's yard to be given yet.

I have sinned old; my lust's a running sore
That drains away my strength. Each morning shout:
'Last night will be the last! At fifty-four
A broken will's a bone that will not knit.
I slip on the loose rubble of remorse
And grasp at tufts of cocksfoot grass that yield,
My belly is a bankrupt's purse.

My mind is a thrice-failed cropping field
Where the missed ridges give out their ecstasy
To weeds that seed through gaps of indiscretion.
Nettles where barley or potatoes should be.
I set my will in Communion and Confession
But still the sore is dribbling – blood, and will
In spite of penance, prayer and canticle.

This was the banal
Beggary that God heard. Was he bored
As men are with the poor? Christ Lord
Hears in the voices of the meanly poor
Homeric utterances, poetry sweeping through.

More pilgrims came that evening
From the pier.
The old ones watched the boats come
And smothered the ridiculous cheer
That breaks, like a hole in pants,
Where the heroic armies advance.

Somebody brought a newspaper
With news of war.
When they lived in Time they knew
What men killed each other for –
Was it something different in the spelling
Of a useless law?

A man under the campanile said:
'Kipper is fish – nice.'
Somebody else talked of Dempsey:
'Greater than Tunney.' Then a girl's voice
Called: 'You'll get cigarettes inside.'

It was six o'clock in the evening.
Robert sat looking over the lake
Seeing the green islands that were his morning hope
And his evening despair.

The sharp knife of Jansen
Cuts all the green branches,
Not sunlight comes in
But the hot-iron sin
Branding the shame
Of a beast in the Name
Of Christ on the breast
Of a child of the West.
It was this he had read.
All day he was smitten
By this foul legend written
In the fields, in the skies,
In the sanctuaries.
But now the green tree
Of humanity
Was leafing again
Forgiveness of sin.
A shading hand over
The brow of the lover.

And as the hours of Lough Derg's time
Stretch long enough to hold a generation
He sat beside her and promised that no word
Of what he knew should ever be heard.
The bell at nine o'clock closed the last station,
The pilgrims kissed goodbye to stone and clay.
The Prior had declared the end of day.

Morning from the hostel windows was like the morning
In some village street after a dance carouse,
Debauchees of Venus and Bacchus
Half-alive stumbling wearily out of a bleary house.
So these pilgrims stumbled below in the sun
Out of God's public-house.

The Mass was said.
Pilgrims smiled at one another
How good God was
How much a loving Father!
How wonderful the punishing stones were!
Another hour and the boats will sail
Into the port of Time.
Are you not glad you came?

John Flood stared at the sky
And shook his proud head knowingly.
No storm, nor rain.
The boats are ready to sail.

The monk appears once more
Not trailing his robe as before
But different, his pride gone,
Green hope growing where the feet of Pan
Had hoofed the grass.
Lough Derg, St Patrick's Purgatory in Donegal,
Christendom's purge. Heretical
Around the edges: the centre's hard
As the commonsense of a flamboyant bard.
The twentieth century blows across it now
But deeply it has kept an ancient vow.
It knows the secret of pain –
O moralist, your preaching is in vain
To tell men of the germ in the grain.

All happened on Lough Derg as it is written
In June nineteen forty-two
When the Germans were fighting outside Rostov.
The poet wrote it down as best he knew
As integral and completed as the emotion
Of men and women cloaking a burning emotion
In the rags of the commonplace, will permit him.

He too was one of them. He too denied
The half of him that was his pride
Yet found it waiting, and the half untrue
Of this story is his pride's rhythm.

The turnips were a-sowing in the fields around Pettigo
As our train passed through.
A horse-cart stopped near the eye of the railway bridge.
By Monaghan and Cavan and Dundalk
By Bundoran and by Omagh the pilgrims went
And three sad people had found the key to the lock
Of God's delight in disillusionment.

Advent

We have tested and tasted too much, lover –
Through a chink too wide there comes in no wonder.
But here in this Advent-darkened room
Where the dry black bread and the sugarless tea
Of penance will charm back the luxury
Of a child's soul, we'll return to Doom
The knowledge we stole but could not use.

And the newness that was in every stale thing
When we looked at it as children: the spirit-shocking
Wonder in a black slanting Ulster hill
Or the prophetic astonishment in the tedious talking
Of an old fool will awake for us and bring
You and me to the yard gate to watch the whins
And the bog-holes, cart-tracks, old stables where Time
    begins.

O after Christmas we'll have no need to go searching
For the difference that sets an old phrase burning –
We'll hear it in the whispered argument of a churning
Or in the streets where the village boys are lurching.
And we'll hear it among simple decent men too
Who barrow dung in gardens under trees,
Wherever life pours ordinary plenty.
Won't we be rich, my love and I, and please
God we shall not ask for reason's payment,
The why of heart-breaking strangeness in dreeping
    hedges
Nor analyse God's breath in common statement.
We have thrown into the dust-bin the clay-minted
    wages
Of pleasure, knowledge and the conscious hour –
And Christ comes with a January flower.

Consider the Grass Growing

Consider the grass growing
As it grew last year and the year before,
Cool about the ankles like summer rivers
When we walked on a May evening through the
    meadows
To watch the mare that was going to foal.

Peace

And sometimes I am sorry when the grass
Is growing over the stones in quiet hollows
And the cocksfoot leans across the rutted cart-pass
That I am not the voice of country fellows
Who now are standing by some headland talking
Of turnips and potatoes or young corn
Or turf banks stripped for victory.
Here Peace is still hawking
His coloured combs and scarves and beads of horn.

Upon a headland by a whinny hedge
A hare sits looking down a leaf-lapped furrow
There's an old plough upside-down on a weedy ridge
And someone is shouldering home a saddle-harrow.
Out of that childhood country what fools climb
To fight with tyrants Love and Life and Time?

Threshing Morning

On an apple-ripe September morning
Through the mist-chill fields I went
With a pitchfork on my shoulder
Less for use than for devilment.

The threshing mill was set-up, I knew,
In Cassidy's haggard last night,
And we owed them a day at the threshing
Since last year. O it was delight

To be paying bills of laughter
And chaffy gossip in kind
With work thrown in to ballast
The fantasy-soaring mind.

As I crossed the wooden bridge I wondered
As I looked into the drain
If ever a summer morning should find me
Shovelling up eels again.

And I thought of the wasps' nest in the bank
And how I got chased one day
Leaving the drag and the scraw-knife behind,
How I covered my face with hay.

The wet leaves of the cocksfoot
Polished my boots as I
Went round by the glistening bog-holes
Lost in unthinking joy.

I'll be carrying bags today, I mused,
The best job at the mill
With plenty of time to talk of our loves
As we wait for the bags to fill . . .

Maybe Mary might call round . . .
And then I came to the haggard gate,
And I knew as I entered that I had come
Through fields that were part of no earthly estate.

A Wreath for Tom Moore's Statue

The cowardice of Ireland is in his statue,
No poet's honoured when they wreathe this stone,
An old shopkeeper who has dealt in the marrow-bone
Of his neighbours looks at you.
Dim-eyed, degenerate, he is admiring his god,
The bank-manager who pays his monthly confession,
The tedious narrative of a mediocrity's passion,
The shallow, safe sins that never become a flood
To sweep themselves away. From under
His coat-lapels the vermin creep as Joyce
Noted in passing on his exile's way.
In the wreathing of this stone now I wonder
If there is not somehow the worship of the lice
That crawl upon the seven-deadened clay.

They put a wreath upon the dead
For the dead will wear the cap of any racket,
The corpse will not put his elbows through his jacket
Or contradict the words some liar has said.
The corpse can be fitted out to deceive –
Fake thoughts, fake love, fake ideal,
And rogues can sell its guaranteed appeal,
Guaranteed to work and never come alive.
The poet would not stay poetical
And his humility was far from being pliable,
Voluptuary tomorrow, today ascetical,
His morning gentleness was the evening's rage.
But here we give you death, the old reliable
Whose white blood cannot blot the respectable page.

Some clay the lice have stirred
Falls now for ever into hell's lousy hollows.

The terrible peace is that follows
The annihilation of the flesh-rotted word.
But hope! the poet comes again to build
A new city high above lust and logic,
The trucks of language overflow and magic
At every turn of the living road is spilled.

The sense is over-sense. No need more
To analyse, to controvert or turn
The laugh against the cynic's leer of power.
In his own city now he lives before
The clay earth was made, an Adam never born,
His light unprisoned in a dinner-hour.

Pegasus

My soul was an old horse
Offered for sale in twenty fairs.
I offered him to the Church – the buyers
Were little men who feared his unusual airs.
One said: 'Let him remain unbid
In the wind and rain and hunger
Of sin and we will get him –
With the winkers thrown in – for nothing.'

Then the men of State looked at
What I'd brought for sale.
One minister, wondering if
Another horse-body would fit the tail
That he'd kept for sentiment –
The relic of his own soul –
Said, 'I will graze him in lieu of his labour.'
I lent him for a week or more
And he came back a hurdle of bones,

Starved, overworked, in despair.
I nursed him on the roadside grass
To shape him for another fair.

I lowered my price. I stood him where
The broken-winded, spavined stand
And crooked shopkeepers said that he
Might do a season on the land –
But not for high-paid work in towns.
He'd do a tinker, possibly.
I begged, 'O make some offer now,
A soul is a poor man's tragedy.
He'll draw your dungiest cart,' I said,
'Show you short cuts to Mass,
Teach weather lore, at night collect
Bad debts from poor men's grass.'

                                     And they would not.

                    Where the
Tinkers quarrel I went down
With my horse, my soul.
I cried, 'Who will bid me half a crown?'
From their rowdy bargaining
Not one turned. 'Soul,' I prayed,
'I have hawked you through the world
Of Church and State and meanest trade.
But this evening, halter off,
Never again will it go on.
On the south side of ditches
There is grazing of the sun.
No more haggling with the world . . .'

As I said these words he grew
Wings upon his back. Now I may ride him
Every land my imagination knew.

Memory of Brother Michael

It would never be morning, always evening,
Golden sunset, golden age –
When Shakespeare, Marlowe and Jonson were writing
The future of England page by page
A nettle-wild grave was Ireland's stage.

It would never be spring, always autumn
After a harvest always lost,
When Drake was winning seas for England
We sailed in puddles of the past
Chasing the ghost of Brendan's mast.

The seeds among the dust were less than dust,
Dust we sought, decay,
The young sprout rising smothered in it,
Cursed for being in the way –
And the same is true today.

Culture is always something that was,
Something pedants can measure,
Skull of bard, thigh of chief,
Depth of dried-up river.
Shall we be thus for ever?
Shall we be thus for ever?

Bluebells for Love

There will be bluebells growing under the big trees
And you will be there and I will be there in May;
For some other reason we both will have to delay
The evening in Dunshaughlin – to please
Some imagined relation,
So both of us came to walk through that plantation.

We will be interested in the grass,
In an old bucket-hoop, in the ivy that weaves
Green incongruity among dead leaves,
We will put on surprise at carts that pass –
Only sometimes looking sideways at the bluebells in the
        plantation
And never frighten them with too wild an exclamation.

We will be wise, we will not let them guess
That we are watching them or they will pose
A mere façade like boys
Caught out in virtue's naturalness.
We will not impose on the bluebells in that plantation
Too much of our desire's adulation.

We will have other loves – or so they'll think;
The primroses or the ferns or the briars,
Or even the rusty paling wires,
Or the violets on the sunless sorrel bank.
Only as an aside the bluebells in the plantation
Will mean a thing to our dark contemplation.

We'll know love little by little, glance by glance.
Ah, the clay under these roots is so brown!
We'll steal from Heaven while God is in the town –
I caught an angel smiling in a chance
Look through the tree-trunks of the plantation
As you and I walked slowly to the station.

Temptation in Harvest

A poplar leaf was spiked upon a thorn
Above the hedge like a flag of surrender
That the year hung out. I was afraid to wonder
At capitulation in a field of corn.
The yellow posies in the headland grass
Paraded up and down in loud apparel;
If I could search their hearts I'd find a moral
For men and women – but I let them pass.
Hope guarantees the poor that they will be
Masters at haw-time when the robins are
Courageous as a crow or water-hen. O see
There someone on an ash tree's limb
Sawing a stick for a post or a drilling-bar!
I wish that I this moment were with him!

I should not have wished, should not have seen how white
The wings of thistle seeds are, and how gay
Amoral Autumn gives her soul away
And every maidenhead without a fight.
I turned to the stubble of the oats,
Knowing that clay could still seduce my heart
After five years of pavements raised to art.
O the devilry of the fields! petals that goats
Have plucked from rose bushes of vanity!
But here! a small blue flower creeping over
On a trailing stem across an inch-wide chasm.
Even here wild gods have set a net for sanity.
Where can I look and not become a lover
Terrified at each recurring spasm?

This time of the year mind worried
About the threshing of the corn and whether
The yellow streaks in the sunset were for fine weather.

The sides of the ricks were letting in; too hurried
We built them to beat the showers that were flying
All day. 'It's raining in Drummeril now,'
We'd speculate, half happy to think how
Flat on the ground a neighbour's stooks were lying.
Each evening combing the ricks like a lover's hair,
Gently combing the butt-ends to run the rain,
Then running to the gate to see if there
Was anybody travelling on the train.
The Man in the Moon has water on the brain!
I love one! but my ricks are more my care.

An old woman whispered from a bush: 'Stand in
The shadow of the ricks until she passes;
You cannot eat what grows upon Parnassus –
And she is going there as sure as sin.'
I saw her turn her head as she went down
The blackberry lane-way, and I knew
In my heart that only what we love is true –
And not what loves us, we should make our own.
I stayed in indecision by the gate,
As Christ in Gethsemane, to guess
Into the morrow and the day after,
And tried to keep from thinking on the fate
Of those whom beauty tickles into laughter
And leaves them on their backs in muddiness.

The air was drugged with Egypt. Could I go
Over the field to the City of the Kings
Where art, music, letters are the real things?
The stones of the street, the sheds, hedges cried, No.
Earth, earth! I dragged my feet off the ground.
Labourers, animals armed with farm tools,
Ringed me. The one open gap had larch poles
Across it now by memory secured and bound.

The flaggers in the swamp were the reserves
Waiting to lift their dim nostalgic arms
The moment I would move. The noise of carts
Softening into haggards wove new charms.
The simplest memory plays upon the nerves
Symphonies that break down what the will asserts.

O Life, forgive me for my sins! I can hear
In the elm by the potato-pits a thrush;
Rain is falling on the Burning Bush
Where God appeared. Why now do I fear
That clear in the sky where the Evening Star is born?
Why does the inconsequential gabble
Of an old man among the hills so trouble
My thoughts this September evening? Now I turn
Away from the ricks, the sheds, the cabbage garden,
The stones of the street, the thrush song in the tree,
The potato-pits, the flaggers in the swamp;
From the country heart that hardly learned to harden,
From the spotlight of an old-fashioned kitchen lamp
I go to follow her who winked at me.

Father Mat

[I]

                    In a meadow
Beside the chapel three boys were playing football.
At the forge door an old man was leaning
Viewing a hunter-hoe. A man could hear
If he listened to the breeze the fall of wings –
How wistfully the sin-birds come home!

It was Confession Saturday, the first
Saturday in May; the May Devotions
Were spread like leaves to quieten
The excited armies of conscience.
The knife of penance fell so like a blade
Of grass that no one was afraid.

Father Mat came slowly walking, stopping to
Stare through gaps at ancient Ireland sweeping
In again with all its unbaptized beauty:
The calm evening,
The whitethorn blossoms,
The smell from ditches that were not Christian.
The dancer that dances in the hearts of men cried:
Look! I have shown this to you before –
The rags of living surprised
The joy in things you cannot forget.

His heavy hat was square upon his head,
Like a Christian Brother's;
His eyes were an old man's watery eyes,
Out of his flat nose grew spiky hairs.
He was a part of the place,
Natural as a round stone in a grass field;
He could walk through a cattle fair
And the people would only notice his odd spirit there.

His curate passed on a bicycle –
He had the haughty intellectual look
Of the man who never reads in brook or book;
A man designed
To wear a mitre,
To sit on committees –
For will grows strongest in the emptiest mind.

The old priest saw him pass
And, seeing, saw

Himself a medieval ghost.
Ahead of him went Power,
One who was not afraid when the sun opened a flower,
Who was never astonished
At a stick carried down a stream
Or at the undying difference in the corner of a field.

[II]

The Holy Ghost descends
At random like the muse
On wise man and fool,
And why should poet in the twilight choose?

Within the dim chapel was the grey
Mumble of prayer
To the Queen of May –
The Virgin Mary with the schoolgirl air.

Two guttering candles on a brass shrine
Raised upon the wall
Monsters of despair
To terrify deep into the soul.

Through the open door the hum of rosaries
Came out and blended with the homing bees.
                    The trees
Heard nothing stranger than the rain or the wind
Or the birds –
But deep in their roots they knew a seed had sinned.

In the graveyard a goat was nibbling at a yew,
The cobbler's chickens with anxious looks
Were straggling home through nettles, over graves.
A young girl down a hill was driving cows
To a corner at the gable-end of a roofless house.

Cows were milked earlier,
The supper hurried,
Hens shut in,
Horses unyoked,
And three men shaving before the same mirror.

[III]

The trip of iron tips on tile
Hesitated up the middle aisle,
Heads that were bowed glanced up to see
Who could this last arrival be.

Murmur of women's voices from the porch,
Memories of relations in the graveyard.
On the stem
Of memory imaginations blossom.

In the dim
Corners in the side seats faces gather,
Lit up now and then by a guttering candle
And the ghost of day at the window.
A secret lover is saying
Three Hail Marys that she who knows
The ways of women will bring
Cathleen O'Hara (he names her) home to him.
Ironic fate! Cathleen herself is saying
Three Hail Marys to her who knows
The ways of men to bring
Somebody else home to her –
'O may he love me.'
What is the Virgin Mary now to do?

[IV]

From a confessional
The voice of Father Mat's absolving
Rises and falls like a briar in the breeze.
As the sins pour in the old priest is thinking
His fields of fresh grass, his horses, his cows,
His earth into the fires of Purgatory.
It cools his mind.
'They confess to the fields,' he mused,
'They confess to the fields and the air and the sky,'
And forgiveness was the soft grass of his meadow by the
 river;
His thoughts were walking through it now.

His human lips talked on:
'My son,
Only the poor in spirit shall wear the crown;
Those down
Can creep in the low door
On to Heaven's floor.'

The Tempter had another answer ready:
'Ah lad, upon the road of life
'Tis best to dance with Chance's wife
And let the rains that come in time
Erase the footprints of the crime.'

The dancer that dances in the hearts of men
Tempted him again:
'Look! I have shown you this before;
From this mountain-top I have tempted Christ
With what you see now
Of beauty – all that's music, poetry, art
In things you can touch every day.

I broke away
And rule all dominions that are rare;
I took with me all the answers to every prayer
That young men and girls pray for: love, happiness,
    riches –'
O Tempter! O Tempter!

[V]

As Father Mat walked home
Venus was in the western sky
And there were voices in the hedges:
'God the Gay is not the Wise.'

'Take your choice, take your choice,'
Called the breeze through the bridge's eye.
'The domestic Virgin and Her Child
Or Venus with her ecstasy.'

In Memory of My Mother

I do not think of you lying in the wet clay
Of a Monaghan graveyard; I see
You walking down a lane among the poplars
On your way to the station, or happily

Going to second Mass on a summer Sunday –
You meet me and you say:
'Don't forget to see about the cattle –'
Among your earthiest words the angels stray.

And I think of you walking along a headland
Of green oats in June,
So full of repose, so rich with life –
And I see us meeting at the end of a town

On a fair day by accident, after
The bargains are all made and we can walk
Together through the shops and stalls and markets
Free in the oriental streets of thought.

O you are not lying in the wet clay,
For it is a harvest evening now and we
Are piling up the ricks against the moonlight
And you smile up at us – eternally.

On Raglan Road

(Air: 'The Dawning of the Day')

On Raglan Road on an autumn day I met her first and
knew
That her dark hair would weave a snare that I might
one day rue;
I saw the danger, yet I walked along the enchanted way, ˙
And I said, let grief be a fallen leaf at the dawning of
the day.

On Grafton Street in November we tripped lightly along
the ledge
Of the deep ravine where can be seen the worth of
passion's pledge,
The Queen of Hearts still making tarts and I not making
hay –
O I loved too much and by such by such is happiness
thrown away.

I gave her gifts of the mind I gave her the secret sign
that's known
To the artists who have known the true gods of sound
and stone

And word and tint. I did not stint for I gave her poems
  to say
With her own name there and her own dark hair like
  clouds over fields of May.

On a quiet street where old ghosts meet I see her walking
  now
Away from me so hurriedly my reason must allow
That I had wooed not as I should a creature made of
  clay –
When the angel woos the clay he'd lose his wings at the
  dawn of day.

No Social Conscience

He was an egoist with an unsocial conscience,
And I liked him for it though he was out of favour
For he seemed to me to be sincere,
Wanting to be no one's but his own saviour.

He lived in a neutral country through a war
And never cut a sod of turf or said
The word 'Emergency' once,
He simply called it 'the war' and that was bad.

He saw the wild witch eyes which are a Nation's
Turned upon the one man who held
Against the gangs of fear his ordinary soul –
He did no public service but lived for himself.

His one enthusiasm was against the hysteria
Of the dangerous men who are always in procession
Searching for someone to murder or worship –
He never qualified for a directorship or State pension.

The Paddiad

or: The Devil as a Patron of Irish Letters

In the corner of a Dublin pub
This party opens-blub-a-blub
Paddy Whiskey, Rum and Gin
Paddy Three Sheets in the Wind;
Paddy of the Celtic Mist,
Paddy Connemara West,
Chestertonian Paddy Frog
Croaking nightly in the bog.
All the Paddies having fun
Since Yeats handed in his gun.
Every man completely blind
To the truth about his mind.

In their middle sits a fellow
Aged about sixty, bland and mellow;
Saintly silvery locks of hair,
Quiet-voiced as monk at prayer;
Every Paddy's eye is glazed
On this fellow. Mouths amazed
Drink in all his words of praise.
O comic muse descend to see
The devil Mediocrity,
For that is the devil sitting there,
Actually Lucifer.

He has written many Catholic novels,
None of which mention devils:
Daring men, beautiful women,
Nothing about muck or midden,
Wholesome atmosphere – Why must
So-called artists deal with lust?

About the devil's dark intentions
There are some serious misconceptions:
The devil is supposed to be
A nasty man entirely,
Horned and hoofed and fearful gory –
That's his own invented story.

The truth in fact is the reverse
He does not know a single curse;
His forte's praise for what is dead,
Pegasus's Munnings bred.
Far and near he screws his eyes
In search of what will never rise,
Souls that are fusty, safe and dim,
These are the geniuses of the land to him.

Most generous-tempered of the gods
He listens to the vilest odes,
Aye, and not just idle praise!
For these the devil highly pays.
And the crowds for culture cheer and cheer:
'A modern Medici is here,
Never more can it be said
That Irish poets are not fed'
The boys go wild and toast the Joker,
The master of the mediocre.

'A great renaissance is under way'
You can hear the devil say
As into our pub comes a new arrival,
A man who looks the conventional devil:
This is Paddy Conscience, this
Is Stephen Dedalus,
This is Yeats who ranted to
Knave and fool before he knew,
This is Sean O'Casey saying,
Fare thee well to Inishfallen.

He stands on the perimeter of the crowd
Half drunk to show that he's not proud
But willing given half a chance
To play the game with any dunce;
He wears a beaten bedraggled pose
To put the devil at his ease,
But Lucifer sees through the pose
Of drunken talk and dirty clothes;
The casual word that drops by chance
Denotes a dangerous arrogance,
Still sober and alive enough
To blast this world with a puff.

Every Paddy sitting there
Pops up like a startled hare,
Loud ignorings fill each face –
This behaviour's a disgrace,
A savage intruding on our Monday's
Colloquy on trochees, spondees,
And whether Paddy Mist or Frog
Is the greatest singer of the bog.
Hypodermics sourpiss loaded
Are squirted at our foolish poet.
The devil sips his glass of plain
And takes up his theme again:

'My suggestion is for a large bounty
For the best poet in each county.
How many poems, Mist, can you spare
For my new anthology of Clare?
Ten guineas per poem is fair,
But they must definitely be Clare;
Some lyrics in your recent volume
Were influenced by Roscommon.'

Conscience: 'I'm a Clareman more than Mist.'
Mist: 'But essentially a novelist.'
Frog: 'Essentially a man of prose
As any whole-time verseman knows.
I think that Paddy Connemara West
Is worth twenty guineas at least.'
'I agree, Frog,
West is one of the great singers of the bog –
I'll give him twenty guineas, so –'

'Oh, oh, oh,'
Conscience is going mad,
Tearing, raving, using bad
Language in the bar
Where the bards of Ireland are.
Now peace again, they've chucked him out.
Paddy Frog puts down his stout,
Clenches his chubby grocer's fist,
Says: 'I disagree with Mist
That Paddy Connemara West

Is inferior to Stephens at his best –
A Catholic and Gaelic poet,
His last group of poems show it.'
Devil: 'Paddy Connemara gets my vote
As the expresser of the Catholic note.
His pious feeling for the body
And rejection of the shoddy
Mystical cloak that Conscience trails
Places him among the greatest of Gaels;
In my last radio talk I drew
Attention to this Froggish view.

We must bring out a Collected Edition
The money's a minor consideration –
What most we want to bring success

Is an end to petty bitterness,
No more slashing notices in the press
But something broadly generous.
We want an openness of heart –
No Olympian critic saying: depart
From me ye cursed pack of fools,
Only poetasters form schools.
You remember Paddy Conscience:
"Count me out at Mummers' rantings."'

Here news has just come in that Paddy
Conscience lost his latest body,
Dead in Paris –
The devil sighs – 'Shocking news.
I much admired all his views.
A man of genius, generous, kind,
Not a destructive idea in his mind.
My dearest friend! Let's do him proud.
Our wives will make a green silk shroud
To weave him in. The Emerald Isle
Must bury him in tourist style.

A broadcast on his work might be,
A reading of his poetry.
The Government will give a grant
To build a worthy monument,
I know the Minister involved,
The cost will readily be halved.
Before we part let's make a date
To meet tomorrow night at eight
To make the final funeral plans,
For this will be Ireland seen by France.
This is the window of our shop.
Paddy Mist might do an ap-
Preciation on the general
Culture of an Irish funeral.'

All the Paddies rise and hurry
Home to write the inside story
Of their friendship for the late
Genius who was surely great;
Recall his technical innovations,
His domestic life, his patience
With the humblest aspirant
On the literary bent.

All his hunger was imagined,
Never was a falser legend,
He could make whenever he chose
A fortune out of verse or prose.
Irish women spirituelles
Ran from race-tracks at his spell,
Left the beds of jockeys, actors –
These may be considered factors.

The group's dispersed. The devil stays,
Some discontent in his face.
Already he can see another
Conscience coming on to bother
Ireland with muck and anger,
Ready again to die of hunger,
Condemnatory and uncivil –
What a future for a devil!

Spring Day

O Come all ye tragic poets and sing a stave with me –
Give over T. S. Eliot and also W. B.
We'll sing our way through Stephen's Green where
        March has never found
In the growing grass a cadence of the verse of Ezra Pound.

The University girls are like tulip bulbs behind
More luxurious than ever from Holland was consigned,
Those bulbs will shortly break in flower – rayon, silk and
    cotton
And our verbal constipation will be totally forgotten.

Philosophy's a graveyard – only dead men analyse
The reason for existence. Come all you solemn boys
From out your dictionary world and literary gloom –
Kafka's mad, Picasso's sad in Despair's confining room.

O Come all darling poets and try to look more happy,
Forget about sexology as you gossip in the café;
Forget about the books you've read and the inbred verses
    there
Forget about the Kinsey Report and take a mouthful of air.

The world began this morning, God-dreamt and full of birds,
The fashion shops were glorious with the new collection of
    words.
And Love was practising phrases in young balladry –
Ten thousand years must pass before the birth of Psychology.

O Come all ye gallant poets – to know it doesn't matter
Is Imagination's message – break out but do not scatter.
Ordinary things wear lovely wings – the peacock's body's
    common.
O Come all ye youthful poets and try to be more human.

Ante-Natal Dream

    I only know that I was there
    With hayseed in my hair
    Lying on the shady side
    Of a haycock in July.

A crowd was pressing round
My body on the ground
Prising the lids of my eyes –
Open and you'll be wise.

The sky that roared with bees,
The row of poplar trees
Along the stream struck deep
And would not let me sleep.

A boortree tried hard to
Let me see it grow,
Mere notice was enough,
She would take care of love.

A clump of nettles cried:
We'll saturate your pride
Till you are oozing with
The richness of our myth;

For we are all you'll know
No matter where you go –
Every insect, weed
Kept singing in my head.

Thistle, ragwort, bluebottle,
Cleg that maddens cattle
Were crowding round me there
With hayseed in my hair.

Bank Holiday

Nineteen-fifty was the year
The August Bank Holiday that I was here
Sitting in my room alone
Conscious of a season gone;

Ultimate failure straggling up
Through the barren daydream crop.
I must not defer the date
For a meeting with my fate.

There he comes your alter ego
Past the Waterloo and Searson's
With a silly gaping mouth
Sucking smiles from every slut,
Sure that this is Heaven's high manna –
God is good to Patrick Kavanagh,
Building like a rejected lover
Dust into an ivory tower.

In the pubs for seven years
Men have given him their ears,
Buying the essence of his heart
With a porter-perfumed fart.
Make him turn his pockets out
And his seven harvests count.
Spread out the vain collection –
Not a ha'penny of affection.

Knock him to the ground for he
Is your sister Vanity,
Is your brother Clown
Exhibited for a sneering town.
He's your son who's named Tomorrow,
Kill him, kill Remorse, your mother,
Be the father of your fate
On this nineteen-fifty date.

Irish Poets Open Your Eyes

Irish poets open your eyes,
Even Cabra can surprise;
Try the dog-tracks now and then –
Shelbourne Park and crooked men.

Could you ever pray at all
In the Pro-Cathedral
Till a breath of simpleness
Freed your Freudian distress?

Enter in and be a part
Of the world's frustrated heart,
Drive the golf ball of despair,
Superdance away your care.

Be ordinary,
Be saving up to marry.
Kiss her in the alleyway,
Part – 'Same time, same place' and go.

Learn repose on Boredom's bed,
Deep, anonymous, unread
And the god of Literature
Will touch a moment to endure.

To be Dead

To be dead is to stop believing in
The masterpieces we will begin tomorrow;
To be an exile is to be a coward,
To know that growth has stopped,
That whatever is done is the end;

Correct the proofs over and over,
Rewrite old poems again and again,
Tell lies to yourself about your achievement:
Ten printed books on the shelves.
Though you know that no one loves you for
What you have done,
But for what you might do.

And you perhaps take up religion bitterly
Which you laughed at in your youth,
Well not actually laughed
But it wasn't your kind of truth.

Kerr's Ass

We borrowed the loan of Kerr's big ass
To go to Dundalk with butter,
Brought him home the evening before the market
An exile that night in Mucker.

We heeled up the cart before the door,
We took the harness inside –
The straw-stuffed straddle, the broken breeching
With bits of bull-wire tied;

The winkers that had no choke-band,
The collar and the reins . . .
In Ealing Broadway, London Town
I name their several names

Until a world comes to life –
Morning, the silent bog,
And the god of imagination waking
In a Mucker fog.

Who Killed James Joyce?

Who killed James Joyce?
I, said the commentator,
I killed James Joyce
For my graduation.

What weapon was used
To slay mighty Ulysses?
The weapon that was used
Was a Harvard thesis.

How did you bury Joyce?
In a broadcast Symposium,
That's how we buried Joyce
To a tuneful encomium.

Who carried the coffin out?
Six Dublin codgers
Led into Langham Place
By W. R. Rodgers.

Who said the burial prayers? –
Please do not hurt me –
Joyce was no Protestant,
Surely not Bertie?

Who killed Finnegan?
I, said a Yale-man,
I was the man who made
The corpse for the wake man.

And did you get high marks,
The Ph.D.?
I got the B.Litt.
And my master's degree.

Did you get money
For your Joycean knowledge?
I got a scholarship
To Trinity College.

I made the pilgrimage
In the Bloomsday swelter
From the Martello Tower
To the cabby's shelter.

Auditors In

[I]

The problem that confronts me here
Is to be eloquent yet sincere;
Let myself rip and not go phoney
In an inflated testimony.
Is verse an entertainment only?
Or is it a profound and holy
Faith that cries the inner history
Of the failure of man's mission?
Should it be my job to mention
Precisely how I chanced to fail
Through a cursed ideal?
Write down here: he knew what he wanted –
Evilest knowledge ever haunted
Man when he can picture clear
Just what he is searching for.

A car, a big suburban house,
Half secret that he might not lose
The wild attraction of the poor
But proud, the fanatic lure

97

For women of the poet's way
And diabolic underlay;
The gun of pride can bring them down
At twenty paces in the town –
For what? the tragedy is this:
Pride's gunman hesitates to kiss.

A romantic Rasputin
Praying at the heart of sin.
He cannot differentiate
Say if he does not want to take
From moral motives or because
Nature has ideal in her laws.

But to get down to the factual –
You are not homosexual.
And yet you live without a wife,
A most disorganized sort of life.
You've not even bred illegitimates –
A lonely lecher whom the fates
By a financial trick castrates.

You're capable of an intense
Love that is experience.
Remember how your heart was moved
And youth's eternity was proved
When you saw a young girl going to Mass
On a weekday morning as
You yourself used to go
Down to church from Ednamo.
Your imagination still enthuses
Over the dandelions at Willie Hughes'
And these are equally valid
For urban epic, peasant ballad.
Not mere memory but the Real

Poised in the poet's commonweal.
And you must take yourself in hand
And dig and ditch your authentic land.

Wake up, wake up and compromise
On the non-essential sides
Love's round you in a rapturous bevy
But you are bankrupt by the levy
Imposed upon the ideal:
Her Cheshire-cat smile surmounts the wall.
She smiles 'Wolf, wolf, come be my lover'
Unreal you find and yet you never
Catch on. One cannot but feel sorry,
For the ideal is purgatory.
Yet do not be too much dismayed
It's on your hand the humble trade
Of versing that can easily
Restore your equanimity
And lay the looney ghosts that goad
The savages of Pembroke Road . . .
Bow down here and thank your God.

[II]

After the prayer I am ready to enter my heart
Indifferent to the props of a reputation:
Some feeble sallies of a peasant plantation,
The rotten shafts of a remembered cart
Holding up the conscious crust of art.
No quiet corner here for contemplation,
No roots of faith to give my angry passion
Validity. I at the bottom will start
Try to ignore the shame-reflecting eyes
Of worshippers who made their god too tall
To share their food or do the non-stupendous,
They gave him for exploring empty skies

99

Instead of a little room where he might write for
Men too real to live by vapid legends.

Away, away on wings like Joyce's
Mother Earth is putting my brand new clothes in order
Praying, she says, that I no more ignore her
Yellow buttons she found in fields at bargain prices.
Kelly's Big Bush for a button-hole. Surprises
In every pocket – the stream at Connolly's corner,
Myself at Annavackey on the Armagh border,
Or calm and collected in a calving crisis.
Not sad at all as I float away, away
With Mother keeping me to the vernacular.
I have a home to return to now. O blessing
For the return in Departure. Somewhere to stay
Doesn't matter. What is distressing
Is waking eagerly to go nowhere in particular.

From the sour soil of a town where all roots canker
I turn away to where the Self reposes
The placeless Heaven that's under all our noses
Where we're shut off from all the barren anger,
No time for self-pitying melodrama,
A million Instincts know no other uses
Than all day long to feed and charm the Muses
Till they become pure positive. O hunger
Where all have mouths of desire and none
Is willing to be eaten! I am so glad
To come so accidentally upon
My Self at the end of a tortuous road
And have learned with surprise that God
Unworshipped withers to the Futile One.

Innocence

They laughed at one I loved –
The triangular hill that hung
Under the Big Forth. They said
That I was bounded by the whitethorn hedges
Of the little farm and did not know the world.
But I knew that love's doorway to life
Is the same doorway everywhere.

Ashamed of what I loved
I flung her from me and called her a ditch
Although she was smiling at me with violets.

But now I am back in her briary arms
The dew of an Indian Summer morning lies
On bleached potato-stalks –
What age am I?

I do not know what age I am,
I am no mortal age;
I know nothing of women,
Nothing of cities,
I cannot die
Unless I walk outside these whitethorn hedges.

Epic

I have lived in important places, times
When great events were decided: who owned
That half a rood of rock, a no-man's land
Surrounded by our pitchfork-armed claims.
I heard the Duffys shouting 'Damn your soul'

And old McCabe stripped to the waist, seen
Step the plot defying blue cast-steel –
'Here is the march along these iron stones'
That was the year of the Munich bother. Which
Was most important? I inclined
To lose my faith in Ballyrush and Gortin
Till Homer's ghost came whispering to my mind
He said: I made the *Iliad* from such
A local row. Gods make their own importance.

On Looking into E. V. Rieu's Homer

Like Achilles you had a goddess for mother,
For only the half-god can see
The immortal in things mortal;
The far-frightened surprise in a crow's flight
Or the moonlight
That stays for ever in a tree.

In stubble fields the ghosts of corn are
The important spirits the imagination heeds.
Nothing dies; there are no empty
Spaces in the cleanest-reaped fields.

It was no human weakness when you flung
Your body prostrate on a cabbage drill –
Heart-broken with Priam for Hector ravaged;
You did not know why you cried,
This was the night he died –
Most wonderful-horrible
October evening among those cabbages.

The intensity that radiated from
The Far Field Rock – you afterwards denied –
Was the half-god seeing his half-brothers
Joking on the fabulous mountain-side.

God in Woman

Now I must search till I have found my God –
Not in an orphanage. He hides
In no humanitarian disguise,
A derelict upon a barren bog;
But in some fantastically ordinary incog:
Behind a well-bred convent girl's eyes,
Or wrapped in middle-class felicities
Among the women in a coffee shop.
Surely my God is feminine, for Heaven
Is the generous impulse, is contented
With feeding praise to the good. And all
Of these that I have known have come from women.
While men the poet's tragic light resented,
The spirit that is Woman caressed his soul.

I Had a Future

O I had a future
A future.

Gods of the imagination bring back to life
The personality of those streets,
Not any streets
But the streets of nineteen forty.

Give the quarter-seeing eyes I looked out of
The animal-remembering mind
The fog through which I walked towards the mirage
That was my future.

The women I was to meet
They were nowhere within sight.

And then the pathos of the blind soul,
Who without knowing stands in its own kingdom.

Bring me a small detail
How I felt about money,
Not frantic as later,
There was the future.

Show me the stretcher-bed I slept on
In a room on Drumcondra Road.
Let John Betjeman call for me in a car.

It is summer and the eerie beat
Of madness in Europe trembles the
Wings of the butterflies along the canal.

O I had a future.

Wet Evening in April

The birds sang in the wet trees
And as I listened to them it was a hundred years from now
And I was dead and someone else was listening to them.
But I was glad I had recorded for him the melancholy.

A Ballad

O cruel are the women of Dublin's fair city
They smile out of cars and are gone in a flash,
You know they are charming and gay in their hearts
And would laugh as vivaciously buried in chaff
As they would underneath a pink shower of confetti.

I know one in Baggot Street, a medical student
Unless I am greatly mistaken is she;
Her smile plays a tune on my trembling psyche
At thirty yards range, but she passes by me
In a frost that would make Casanova be prudent.

It's the same everywhere – the wish without will,
And it tortures, yet I would not change it for all
The women from Bond Street right down to The Mall,
For wealth is potential, not the readies at call,
I say as I walk down from Baggot Street Bridge.

Having Confessed

Having confessed he feels
That he should go down on his knees and pray
For forgiveness for his pride, for having
Dared to view his soul from the outside.
Lie at the heart of the emotion, time
Has its own work to do. We must not anticipate
Or awaken for a moment. God cannot catch us
Unless we stay in the unconscious room
Of our hearts. We must be nothing,
Nothing that God may make us something.
We must not touch the immortal material
We must not daydream tomorrow's judgement –
God must be allowed to surprise us.
We have sinned, sinned like Lucifer
By this anticipation. Let us lie down again
Deep in anonymous humility and God
May find us worthy material for His hand.

If Ever You Go To Dublin Town

If ever you go to Dublin town
In a hundred years or so
Inquire for me in Baggot Street
And what I was like to know.
O he was a queer one
Fol dol the di do,
He was a queer one
I tell you.

My great-grandmother knew him well,
He asked her to come and call
On him in his flat and she giggled at the thought
Of a young girl's lovely fall.
O he was dangerous
Fol dol the di do,
He was dangerous
I tell you.

On Pembroke Road look out for my ghost
Dishevelled with shoes untied,
Playing through the railings with little children
Whose children have long since died.
O he was a nice man
Fol dol the di do,
He was a nice man
I tell you.

Go into a pub and listen well
If my voice still echoes there,
Ask the men what their grandsires thought
And tell them to answer fair.
O he was eccentric
Fol dol the di do,
He was eccentric
I tell you.

He had the knack of making men feel
As small as they really were
Which meant as great as God had made them
But as males they disliked his air.
O he was a proud one
Fol dol the di do,
He was a proud one
I tell you.

If ever you go to Dublin town
In a hundred years or so
Sniff for my personality,
Is it vanity's vapour now?
O he was a vain one
Fol dol the di do,
He was a vain one
I tell you.

I saw his name with a hundred others
In a book in the library
It said he had never fully achieved
His potentiality.
O he was slothful
Fol dol the di do,
He was slothful
I tell you.

He knew that posterity has no use
For anything but the soul,
The lines that speak the passionate heart,
The spirit that lives alone.
O he was a lone one
Fol dol the di do,
Yet he lived happily
I tell you.

After Forty Years of Age

There was a time when a mood recaptured was enough
Just to be able to hold momentarily November in the
    woods
Or a street we once made our own through being in
    love.

But that is not enough now. The job is to answer
    questions
Experience. Tell us what life has taught you. Not just
    about persons –
Which is futile anyway in the long run – but a concrete,
    as it were, essence.

The role is that of prophet and saviour. To smelt in
    passion
The commonplaces of life. To take over the functions of
    a god in a new fashion.
Ah! there is the question to speculate upon in lieu of an
    answer.

The Rowley Mile

As I was walking down a street
Upon a summer's day
A typical girl I chanced to meet
And gathered courage to say:
'I've seen you many, many times
Upon this Rowley Mile
And I'm foolish enough to believe you love
Me for you always smile.'

Well, she gathered herself into a ball
Receding all the time.
She said: 'I beg your pardon,
I do not know what you mean.'
I stammered vainly for the right word,
I said: 'I mean to say
I'm not trying to get off with you
Or anything in that way.'

The street was full of eyes that stared
At something very odd.
I tried to imagine how little means
Such a contretemps to God.
I followed her a few slow yards
'Please just one moment stop'
And then I dashed with urgent tread
Into a corner shop.

As I walked down that sunny street
I was a broken man
Thanks to an Irish girl
Who smiles but is true to the plan
Taught her by Old Gummy Granny –
You must try out your power with a smile,
But come to the test hard reality must
Make the pace on the Rowley Mile.

Cyrano de Bergerac

She kicked a pebble with her toe,
She tapped a railing idly –
And when we met she swerved and took
The corner very widely.
I thought that could be love; I know
The power of the male,
But without an introduction
The thing, she knows, will fail.

And so I planned for many a day
A ruse to soothe convention:
Stare up at numbers over doors
And some vague doctor mention;
Or get myself invited to

Some party where she'd be —
But all these things went down the drain
Of anti-dignity.

And then one day we actually
Did meet by introduction
And I told her with a laugh or two
She had been my distraction.
She told me I was subtle, her
Love distress to note;
She *was* in love and worried
About someone who was not.

And she always thought when looking at
My loving priestly face
That I was one who surely
Could give her love-advice . . .
And from the mirror, going out,
The lecher looked at me
And grinned before resuming
His priestly dignity.

Intimate Parnassus

Men are what they are, and what they do
Is their own business. If they praise
The gods or jeer at them, the gods can not
Be moved, involved or hurt. Serenely
The citizens of Parnassus look on
As Homer tells us, and never laugh
When any mortal has joined the party.
What happens in the small towns –
Hate, love, envy – is not
The concern of the gods. The poet poor,
Or pushed around, or to be hanged, retains
His full reality; and his authority
Is bogus if the sonorous beat is broken
By disturbances in human hearts – his own
Is detached, experimental, subject matter
For ironic analysis, even for pity
As for some stranger's private problem.
It is not cold on the mountain, human women
Fall like ripe fruit while mere men
Are climbing out on dangerous branches
Of banking, insurance and shops; going
To the theatre; becoming
Acquainted with actors; unhappily
Pretending to a knowledge of art.
Poet, you have reason to be sympathetic –
Count them the beautiful unbroken
And then forget them
As things aside from the main purpose
Which is to be
Passive, observing with a steady eye.

On Reading a Book on Common
Wild Flowers

O the prickly sow thistle that grew in the hollow of the
    Near Field
I used it as a high jump coming home in the evening –
A hurdle race over the puce blossoms of the sow thistles.
Am I late?
Am I tired?
Is my heart sealed
From the ravening passion that will eat it out
Till there is not one pure moment left?

O the greater fleabane that grew at the back of the potato-
    pit.
I often trampled through it looking for rabbit burrows!
The burnet saxifrage was there in profusion
And the autumn gentian –
I knew them all by eyesight long before I knew their names.
We were in love before we were introduced.

Let me not moralize or have remorse, for these names
Purify a corner of my mind;
I jump over them and rub them with my hands,
And a free moment appears brand new and spacious
Where I may live beyond the reach of desire.

Narcissus and the Women

Many women circled the prison of Reflection
Where he lay among the flashing mirrors
Hoping somewhere to find some door of Action
By which he might be rescued from his errors.

Irish Stew

Our ancient civilization – and –
This Christian State of Ireland!

He said to open his oration
With protective incantation.

Then, all in the Name of God
He turned on me a beaming broad

Face that twitched with a restive hate,
And this is what that man did state:

You're far too great a genius to
Talk of steak and onions or a stew,

Luxury would ruin your sublime
Imagination in no time.

And domesticity, wife, house, car,
We want you always as you are.

Such things don't fit into the scheme
Of one who dreams the poet's dream.

Your wildness is your great attraction,
You could not be a man of action.

Now, you'll never have to worry how to live –
A man who has so much to give.

My cousin dabbles in verse? but he
Has not your spark of poetry;

Unlike you he has not nobly strained –
But in economics he is trained;

He has a politician's mind
To deal with an ugly world designed;

Knows how to handle you great men,
Artists and masters of the pen,

Can run an office, plan a series
Of lectures for the Cork O'Learys

Or Jesuits of Clongowes College
Because he's got the practical knowledge

And that is why he has been sent
To travel on the Continent

To bring back the secret of great arts
To Kerry and remoter parts.

To spread in Naas and Clonakilty
News of Gigli and R. M. Rilke.

Our last art emissary whored
And that's one reason we can't afford

To risk an important man like you
In the dangerous European stew.

Prelude

Give us another poem, he said
Or they will think your muse is dead;
Another middle-age departure
Of Apollo from the trade of archer.
Bring out a book as soon as you can
To let them see you're a living man,
Whose comic spirit is untamed
Though sadness for a little claimed
The precedence; and tentative

You pulled your punch and wondered if
Old cunning Silence might not be
A better bet than poetry.

You have not got the countenance
To hold the angle of pretence,
That angry bitter look for one
Who knows that art's a kind of fun;
That all true poems laugh inwardly
Out of grief-born intensity.
Dullness alone can get you beat
And so can humour's counterfeit.
You have not got a chance with fraud
And might as well be true to God.

Then link your laughter out of doors
In sunlight past the sick-faced whores
Who chant the praise of love that isn't
And bring their bastards to be Christened
At phoney founts by bogus priests
With rites mugged up by journalists.
Walk past professors looking serious
Fondling an unpublished thesis –
'A child! my child! my darling son'
Some Poets of Nineteen Hundred and One
Note well the face profoundly grave.
An empty mind can house a knave.
Be careful to show no defiance.
They've made pretence into a science:
Card-sharpers of the art committees
Working all the provincial cities,
They cry 'Eccentric' if they hear
A voice that seems at all sincere.
Fold up their table and their gear
And with the money disappear.

But satire is unfruitful prayer,
Only wild shoots of pity there,
And you must go inland and be
Lost in compassion's ecstasy,
Where suffering soars in summer air –
The millstone has become a star.

Count then your blessings, hold in mind
All that has loved you or been kind:
Those women on their mercy missions,
Rescue work with kiss or kitchens,
Perceiving through the comic veil
The poet's spirit in travail.

Gather the bits of road that were
Not gravel to the traveller
But eternal lanes of joy
On which no man who walks can die.
Bring in the particular trees
That caught you in their mysteries.
And love again the weeds that grew
Somewhere specially for you.
Collect the river and the stream
That flashed upon a pensive theme,
And a positive world make,
A world man's world cannot shake,
And do not lose love's resolution
Though face to face with destitution.

If Platitude should claim a place
Do not denounce his humble face;
His sentiments are well-intentioned
He has a part in the larger legend.

So now my gentle tiger burning
In the forest of no-yearning
Walk on serenely, do not mind

That Promised Land you thought to find
Where the worldly-wise and rich take over
The mundane problems of the lover.
Ignore Power's schismatic sect
Lovers alone lovers protect.

Nineteen Fifty-Four

Nineteen Fifty-Four hold on till I try
To formulate some theory about you. A personal
    matter:
My lamp of contemplation you sought to shatter,
To leave me groping in madness under a low sky.
O I wish I could laugh! O I wish I could cry!
Or find some formula, some mystical patter
That would organize a perspective from this hellish
    scatter –
Everywhere I look a part of me is exiled from the I.
Therefore I must tell you before you depart my position;
Making the statement is enough – there are no answers
To any real question. But tonight I cannot sleep;
Two hours ago I heard the late homing dancers.
O Nineteen Fifty-Four you leave and will not listen,
And do not care whether I curse or weep.

The Hospital

A year ago I fell in love with the functional ward
Of a chest hospital: square cubicles in a row
Plain concrete, wash basins – an art lover's woe,
Not counting how the fellow in the next bed snored.
But nothing whatever is by love debarred,
The common and banal her heat can know.
The corridor led to a stairway and below
Was the inexhaustible adventure of a gravelled yard.

This is what love does to things: the Rialto Bridge,
The main gate that was bent by a heavy lorry,
The seat at the back of a shed that was a suntrap.
Naming these things is the love-act and its pledge;
For we must record love's mystery without claptrap,
Snatch out of time the passionate transitory.

Leaves of Grass

When I was growing up and for many years after
I was led to believe that poems were thin
Dreary, irrelevant, well out of the draught of laughter
With headquarters the size of the head of a pin.
I do not wonder now that my mother moaned
To see her beloved son an idiot boy;
He could not see what was before his eyes, the ground
Tumultuous with living, infinite as Cleopatra's variety.
He hit upon the secret door that leads to the heaven
Of human satisfaction, a purpose, and did not know it;

An army of grass blades were at his call, million on
    million
Kept saying to him, we nearly made Whitman a poet.
Years after in Dublin in summer past midnight o'clock
They called to him vainly from kerbstones on Bachelor's
    Walk.

October

O leafy yellowness you create for me
A world that was and now is poised above time,
I do not need to puzzle out Eternity
As I walk this arboreal street on the edge of a town.
The breeze too, even the temperature
And pattern of movement is precisely the same
As broke my heart for youth passing. Now I am sure
Of something. Something will be mine wherever I am.
I want to throw myself on the public street without
    caring
For anything but the prayering that the earth offers.
It is October over all my life and the light is staring
As it caught me once in a plantation by the fox coverts.
A man is ploughing ground for winter wheat
And my nineteen years weigh heavily on my feet.

Requiem for a Mill

They took away the water-wheel,
Scrap-ironed all the corn-mill;
The water now cascades with no
Audience pacing to and fro
Taking in with casual glance
Experience.

The cold wet blustery winter day
And all that's happening will stay
Alive in the mind: the bleak
Water-flushed meadows speak
An enduring story
To a man indifferent in a doorway.

Packaged, pre-cooked flakes have left
A land of that old mill bereft.
The ghosts that were so local coloured
Hiding behind bags of pollard
Have gone from those empty walls.
The weir still curves its waterfalls
But lets them drop in the tailrace
No longer wildly chivalrous.

And with this mention we withdraw
To things above the temporal law.

Birth

We will not hold an inquest on the past –
The Word died, the mistake was made, the sin
Was committed as the wheel turned again
And again, exactly as it had turned last.
In the mornings we made promises to ourselves as the
    fresh
Air of the street gave us that springtime feeling
That is to say, sad hope. Our wills were willing
And plenty of years in the future said, wish your wish.
Yet there was something of the dead past polluting
The New Word we had created out of the water and the
    spirit
And everything seemed over bar the shouting
When out of the holy mouth came angelic grace
And the will that had fought had found new merit
And all sorts of beautiful things appeared in that place.

Question to Life

Surely you would not ask me to have known
Only the passion of primrose banks in May
Which are merely a point of departure for the play
And yearning poignancy when on their own.
Yet when all is said and done a considerable
Portion of living is found in inanimate
Nature, and a man need not feel miserable
If fate should have decided on this plan of it.
Then there is always the passing gift of affection
Tossed from the windows of high charity

In the office girl and civil servant section
And these are no despisable commodity.
So be reposed and praise, praise, praise
The way it happened and the way it is.

Come Dance with Kitty Stobling

No, no, no, I know I was not important as I moved
Through the colourful country, I was but a single
Item in the picture, the namer not the beloved.
O tedious man with whom no gods commingle.
Beauty, who has described beauty? Once upon a time
I had a myth that was a lie but it served:
Trees walking across the crests of hills and my rhyme
Cavorting on mile-high stilts and the unnerved
Crowds looking up with terror in their rational faces.
O dance with Kitty Stobling I outrageously
Cried out-of-sense to them, while their timorous paces
Stumbled behind Jove's page boy paging me.
I had a very pleasant journey, thank you sincerely
For giving me my madness back, or nearly.

Is

The important thing is not
To imagine one ought
Have something to say,
A raison d'être, a plot for the play.
The only true teaching
Subsists in watching
Things moving or just colour
Without comment from the scholar.
To look on is enough
In the business of love.
Casually remark
On a deer running in a park;
Mention water again
Always virginal,
Always original,
It washes out Original Sin.
Name for the future
The everydays of nature
And without being analytic
Create a great epic.
Girls in red blouses,
Steps up to houses,
Sunlight round gables,
Gossip's young fables,
The life of a street.

O wealthy me! O happy state!
With an inexhaustible theme
I'll die in harness,
I'll die in harness with my scheme.

To Hell with Commonsense

More kicks than pence
We get from commonsense
Above its door is writ
All hope abandon. It
Is a bank will refuse a post
Dated cheque of the Holy Ghost.
Therefore I say to hell
With all reasonable
Poems in particular
We want no secular
Wisdom plodded together
By concerned fools. Gather
No moss you rolling stones
Nothing thought out atones
For no flight
In the light.
Let them wear out nerve and bone
Those who would have it that way
But in the end nothing that they
Have achieved will be in the shake up
In the final Wake Up
And I have a feeling
That through the hole in reason's ceiling
We can fly to knowledge
Without ever going to college.

Canal Bank Walk

Leafy-with-love banks and the green waters of the canal
Pouring redemption for me, that I do
The will of God, wallow in the habitual, the banal,
Grow with nature again as before I grew.
The bright stick trapped, the breeze adding a third
Party to the couple kissing on an old seat,
And a bird gathering materials for the nest for the Word
Eloquently new and abandoned to its delirious beat.
O unworn world enrapture me, encapture me in a web
Of fabulous grass and eternal voices by a beech,
Feed the gaping need of my senses, give me ad lib
To pray unselfconsciously with overflowing speech
For this soul needs to be honoured with a new dress
     woven
From green and blue things and arguments that cannot
     be proven.

Dear Folks

Just a line to remind my friends that after much trouble
Of one kind and another I am back in circulation.
I have recovered most of my heirlooms from the humps of
     rubble
That once was the house where I lived in the name of a nation.
And precious little I assure you was worth mind storage:
The images of half a dozen women who fell for the unusual,
For the Is that Is and the laughter-smothered courage,
The poet's. And I also found some crucial
Documents of sad evil that may yet
For all their ugliness and vacuous leers

Fuel the fires of comedy. The main thing is to continue,
To walk Parnassus right into the sunset
Detached in love where pygmies cannot pin you
To the ground like Gulliver. So good luck and cheers.

Song at Fifty

It came as a pleasant surprise
To find experience
Where I had feared that I
Had no such currency,
Had idled to a void
Without a wife or child,
I had been looking at
Fields, gates, lakes, all that
Was part and parcel of
The wild breast of love.
In other fellows' wives
I lived a many lives
And here another cries:
My husband I despise
And truth is my true
Husband is you.

So I take my cloak of gold
And stride across the world
A knight of chivalry
Seeking some devilry
The winter trees rise up
And wave me on, a clap
Of falling rock declares
Enthusiasm; flares
Announce a reception committee

For me entering a city.
And all this for an unthrifty
Man turned of fifty;
An undisciplined person
Through futile excitements arsing
Finds in his spendthrift purse
A bankbook writ in verse
And borrowers of purity
Offering substantial security.
To him who just strayed
Through a lifetime without a trade,
Him, him the ne'er-
Do-well a millionaire.

Freedom

Take me to the top of the high hill
Mount Olympus laughter-roaring unsolemn
Where no one is angry and satirical
About a mortal creature on a tall column.

Lines Written on a Seat on the Grand Canal, Dublin

'Erected to the Memory of Mrs Dermot O'Brien'

O commemorate me where there is water,
Canal water preferably, so stilly
Greeny at the heart of summer. Brother
Commemorate me thus beautifully
Where by a lock niagarously roars
The falls for those who sit in the tremendous silence
Of mid-July. No one will speak in prose
Who finds his way to these Parnassian islands.
A swan goes by head low with many apologies,
Fantastic light looks through the eyes of bridges —
And look! a barge comes bringing from Athy
And other far-flung towns mythologies.
O commemorate me with no hero-courageous
Tomb — just a canal-bank seat for the passer-by.

The Self-Slaved

Me I will throw away.
Me sufficient for the day
The sticky self that clings
Adhesions on the wings.
To love and adventure,
To go on the grand tour
A man must be free
From self-necessity.

See over there
A created splendour

Made by one individual
From things residual
With all the various
Qualities hilarious
Of what
Hitherto was not:

A November mood
As by one man understood;
Familiar, an old custom
Leaves falling, a white frosting
Bringing a sanguine dream
A new beginning with an old theme.

Throw away thy sloth
Self, carry off my wrath
With its self-righteous
Satirizing blotches.
No self, no self-exposure
The weakness of the proser
But undefeatable
By means of the beatable.

I will have love, have love
From anything made of
And a life with a shapely form
With gaiety and charm
And capable of receiving
With grace the grace of living
And wild moments too
Self when freed from you.
Prometheus calls me on.
Prometheus calls me: Son,
We'll both go off together
In this delightful weather.

The One

Green, blue, yellow and red –
God is down in the swamps and marshes
Sensational as April and almost incred-
     ible the flowering of our catharsis.
A humble scene in a backward place
Where no one important ever looked
The raving flowers looked up in the face
Of the One and the Endless, the Mind that has baulked
The profoundest of mortals. A primrose, a violet,
A violent wild iris – but mostly anonymous performers
Yet an important occasion as the Muse at her toilet
Prepared to inform the local farmers
That beautiful, beautiful, beautiful God
Was breathing His love by a cut-away bog.

Yellow Vestment

Lately I have been travelling by a created guidance,
I invented a Superintendent, symbol henceforth vaster
Than Jupiter, Prometheus or a Chinese deity in alabaster.
For love's sake we must only consider whatever widens
The field of the faithful's activity. See over there
Water-lilies waiting to be enchanted by a folk song chanted.
On the road we walk nobody is unwanted;
With no hate in his heart or resentment each may wear
The arrogant air that goes with a yellow vestment.
Do not be worried about what the neighbours will say,
Deliver your judgment, you are independent
Of the man in the pub whose word is essential to happiness,
Who gives you existence. O sing to me some roundelay
And wear with grace the power-invoking habit.

Love in a Meadow

She waved her body in the circle sign
Of love purely born without side;
The earth's contour, she orbited to my pride,
Sin and unsin.
But the critic asking questions ran
From the fright of the dawn
To weep later on an urban lawn
For the undone
God-gifted man.
O the river flowed round and round
The low meadows filled with buttercups
In a place called Toprass.
I was born on high ground.

Miss Universe

I learned, I learned – when one might be inclined
To think, too late, you cannot recover your losses –
I learned something of the nature of God's mind,
Not the abstract Creator but He who caresses
The daily and nightly earth; He who refuses
To take failure for an answer till again and again is worn.
Love is waiting for you, waiting for the violence that she
    chooses
From the tepidity of the common round beyond
    exhaustion or scorn.
What was once is still and there is no need for remorse;
There are no recriminations in Heaven. O the sensual
    throb

Of the explosive body, the tumultuous thighs!
Adown a summer lane comes Miss Universe
She whom no lecher's art can rob
Though she is not the virgin who was wise.

Winter

Christmas, someone mentioned, is almost upon us
And looking out my window I saw that Winter had
    landed
Complete with the grey cloak and the bare tree sonnet.
A scroll of bark hanging down to the knees as he scanned
    it.
The gravel in the yard was pensive annoyed to be
    crunched
As people with problems in their faces drove in in cars
Yet I with such solemnity around me refused to be
    bunched
In fact was inclined to give the go-by to bars.
Yes, there were things in that winter arrival that made
    me
Feel younger, less of a failure, it was actually earlier
Than many people thought; there were possibilities
For love, for South African adventure, for fathering a
    baby
For taking oneself in hand, catching on without a scare
    me, or
Taking part in a world war, joining up at the start of
    hostilities.

Living in the Country

Opening

It was the Warm Summer, that landmark
In a child's mind, an infinite day
Sunlight and burnt grass
Green grasshoppers on the railway slopes
The humming of wild bees
The whole summer during the school holidays
Till the blackberries appeared.
Yes, a tremendous time that summer stands
Beyond the grey finities of normal weather.

The Main Body

It's not nearly as bad as you'd imagine
Living among small farmers in the north of Ireland
They are for the most part the ordinary frightened
Blind brightened, referred to sometimes socially
As the underprivileged.
They cannot perceive Irony or even Satire
They start up with insane faces if
You break the newspaper moral code.
'Language' they screech 'you effing so and so'
And you withdraw into a precarious silence
Organizing in your mind quickly, for the situation is
     tense,
The theological tenets of the press.

There's little you can do about some
Who roar horribly as you enter a bar
Incantations of ugliness, words of half a syllable
Locked in malicious muteness full of glare.
And your dignity thinks of giving up the beer.

But I, trained in the slum pubs of Dublin
Among the most offensive class of all –
The artisans – am equal to this problem;
I let it ride and there is nothing over.
I understand through all these years
That my difference in their company is an intrusion
That tears at the sentimental clichés
They can see my heart squirm when their star rendites
The topmost twenty in the lowered lights.
No sir, I did not come unprepared.

Oddly enough I begin to think of Saint Francis
Moving in this milieu (of his own time of course)
How did he work the oracle?
Was he an old fraud, a non-poet
Who is loved for his non-ness
Like any performer?

I protest here and now and for ever
On behalf of all my peoples who believe in Verse
That my intention is not satire but humaneness
An eagerness to understand more about sad man
Frightened man, the workers of the world
Without being savaged in the process.
Broadness is my aim, a broad road where the many
Can see life easier – generally.

Here I come to a sticky patch
A personal matter that perhaps
Might be left as an unrevealed hinterland
For our own misfortunes are mostly unimportant.
But that wouldn't do.
So with as little embarrassment as possible I tell
How I was done out of a girl,
Not as before by a professional priest but by
The frightened artisan's morality.

It was this way.
She, a shopgirl of nineteen or less
Became infatuated by the old soldier,
The wide travelled, the sin-wise.
Desdemona-Othello idea.
O holy spirit of infatuation
God's gift to his poetic nation!

One day her boss caught her glance.
'You're looking in his eyes' he said.
From then on all the powers of the lower orders –
Perhaps all orders – were used to deprive me of my prize
Agamemnon's Briseis.
It soured me a bit as I had
Everything planned, no need to mention what,
Except that it was August evening under whitethorn
And early blackberries.

In many ways it is a good thing to be cast into exile
Among strangers
Who have no inkling
Of The Other Man concealed
Monstrously musing in a field.
For me they say a Rosary
With many a glossary.

News Item

In Islington for the moment I reside
A hen's race from Cheapside
Where Tom the peeping sun first eyed.

Where Gilpin's horse had bolted
All the traffic halted
The man on board was malted.

And in these romantic lots
I run into Paul Potts
Noticing the pull of roots.

I have taken roots of love
And will find it pain to move.
Betjeman, you've missed much of

The secrets of London while
Old churches you beguile
I'll show you a holier aisle –

The length of Gibson Square
Caught in November's stare.
That would set you to prayer.

Dickens – all the clichés
Revert to the living species
Ideas with the impact of Nietzsche's.

I walk in Islington Green
Finest landscape you ever seen
I'm as happy as I've ever been.

Mermaid Tavern

No System, no Plan,
Yeatsian invention
No all-over
Organizational prover.
Let words laugh
And people be stimulated by our stuff.

Michelangelo's Moses
Is one of the poses
Of Hemingway

Jungle-crashing after prey
Beckett's garbage-can
Contains all our man
Who without fright on his face
Dominates the place
And makes all feel
That all is well.

Yet without smuggery
Or the smirk of buggery
Or any other aid
We have produced our god
And everyone present
Becomes godded and pleasant
Confident, gay –
No remorse that a day
Can show no output
Except from the gut.

In the Name of The Father
The Son and The Mother
We explode
Ridiculously, uncode
A habit and find therein
A successful human being.

Literary Adventures

I am here in a garage in Monaghan.
It is June and the weather is warm,
Just a little bit cloudy. There's the sun again
Lifting to importance my sixteen acre farm.
There are three swallows' nests in the rafters above me
And the first clutches are already flying.

Spread this news, tell all if you love me,
You who knew that when sick I was never dying
(Nae gane, nae gane, nae frae us torn
But taking a rest like John Jordan).

                       Other exclusive
News stories that cannot be ignored:
I climbed Woods' Hill and the elusive
Underworld of the grasses could be heard,
John Lennon shouted across the valley.
Then I saw a New June Moon, quite as stunning
As when young we blessed the sight as something
     holy . . .
Sensational adventure that is only beginning.

For I am taking this evening walk through places
High up among the Six Great Wonders,
The power privileges, the unborn amazes
The unplundered
Where man with no meaning blooms
Large in the eyes of his females:
He doesn't project, nor even assumes
The loss of one necessary believer.
It's as simple as that, it's a matter
Of walking with the little gods, the ignored
Who are so seldom asked to write the letter
Containing the word.
O only free gift! no need for Art any more
When Authority whispers like Tyranny at the end of a
     bar.

That Garage

The lilacs by the gate
The summer sun again
The swallows in and out
Of the garage where I am.
The sounds of land activity
Machinery in gear
This is not longevity
But infinity.
Perhaps a little bit
Too facilely romantic
We must stop and struggle with
A mood that's getting frantic
Getting Georgian
Richard Church and Binyon
O stand and plan
More difficult dominion.

The Same Again

I have my friends, my public and they are waiting
For me to come again as their one and only bard
With a new statement that will repay all the waitment
While I was hitting the bottle hard.
I know it is not right to be light and flippant
There are people in the streets who steer by my star.
There was nothing they could do but view me while I threw
Back large whiskeys in the corner of a smoky bar
And if only I would get drunk it wouldn't be so bad
With a pain in my stomach I wasn't even comic
Swallowing every digestive pill to be had.

Some of my friends stayed faithful but quite a handful
Looked upon it as the end: I could quite safely be
Dismissed a dead loss in the final up toss.
He's finished and that's definitely.

Thank You, Thank You

... Particularly if yourself
Have been left as they call it on the shelf
All God's chillun got wings
So the black Alabaman sings.

Down Grafton Street on Saturdays
Don't grieve like Marcus Aurelius
Who said that though he grew old and grey
The people on the Appian Way
Were always the same pleasant age
Twenty-four on average.

I can never help reflecting
On coming back in another century
From now and feeling comfortable
At a buzzing coffee table,
Students in 2056
With all the old eternal tricks.

The thing that I most glory in
Is this exciting unvarying
Quality that withal
Is completely original.

For what it teaches is just this
We are not alone in our loneliness,
Others have been here and known
Griefs we thought our special own

Problems that we could not solve
Lovers that we could not have
Pleasures that we missed by inches.
Come I'm beginning to get pretentious
Beginning to message forth instead
Of expressing how glad
I am to have lived to feel the radiance
Of a holy hearing audience
And delivered God's commands
Into those caressing hands,
My personality that's to say
All that is mine exclusively.
What wisdom's ours if such there be
Is a flavour of personality.
I thank you and I say how proud
That I have been by fate allowed
To stand here having the joyful chance
To claim my inheritance
For most have died the day before
The opening of that holy door.

Epilogue to a series of lectures given at
University College, Dublin

In Blinking Blankness: Three Efforts

[I]

I am here all morning with the familiar
Blank page in front of me, I have perused
An American anthology for stimulation
But the result is not encouraging as it used
To be when Walter Lowenfel's falling down words

Like ladders excited me to chance my arm
With nouns and verbs.
But the wren, the wren got caught in the furze
And the eagle turned turkey on my farm.

[II]

Last summer I made a world fresh and fair,
(As the daughters of Erin) completely equipped
With everything for the full life. A wealth of experience
Of every kind waiting to be tapped.
I had a story, a career
Shaped like a statesman's for the biographer.
I had done all things in my time
And had not yet reached my prime.

[III]

Nature is not enough, I've used up lanes,
Waters that run in rivers or are stagnant;
But I have no message and the sins
Of no red idea can make me pregnant.
So I sit tight to manufacture
A world word by word-machine-to-live-in structure –
That may in any garden be assembled
Where critics looking through the glass can lecture
On poets – X, Y and Z therein entempled.

One Wet Summer

Another summer, another July
People going on holiday, women in light dresses
How I once jealously feared for them under the printed
    cotton
Limp unresisting to any man's caresses.

I would have one of my own
And then like other men I could make cynical remarks
At the dangers they ran and never be worried about
    summer
And what happens in the shelter of parks.

As it is I praise the rain
For washing out the bank holiday with its moral risks
It is not a nice attitude but it is conditioned by
    circumstances
And by a childhood perverted by Christian moralists.

An Insult

I came to a great house on the edge of a park
Thinking on Yeats's dream great house where all
Nobility was protected by ritual
Though all lay drunk on the floor and in the dark
Tough louts and menial minds in the shrubberies lurk
And negative eunuchs hate in an outer hall.
The poet and lover is sage though from grace he fall
Temporarily. The Evil Barbarian dare not work
The servile spell, the insult of a fool

To which there is no answer but to pray
For guidance through the parks of everyday,
To be silent till the soul itself forgives,
To learn again there is no golden rule
For keeping out of suffering – if one lives.

Personal Problem

To take something as a subject, indifferent
To personal affection, I have been considering
Some old saga as an instrument
To play upon without the person suffering
From the tiring years. But I can only
Tell of my problem without solving
Anything. If I could rewrite a famous tale
Or perhaps return to a midnight calving,
This cow sacred on a Hindu scale –
So there it is my friends. What am I to do
With the void growing more awful every hour?
I lacked a classical discipline. I grew
Uncultivated and now the soil turns sour,
Needs to be revived by a power not my own,
Heroes enormous who do astounding deeds –
Out of this world. Only thus can I attune
To despair an illness like winter alone in Leeds.

Notes

Address to an Old Wooden Gate

First publication and source text: the *Dundalk Democrat* (2 February 1929).

Kavanagh contributed a number of poems to a poetry competition in a national newspaper, the *Irish Weekly Independent*, between September 1928 and June 1929. This poem, printed in a local newspaper, is the best of his earliest published verse.

'scringes' is a colloquial word meaning 'rasping sounds'.

Pygmalion

First publication: *Collected Poems* (1964).

Source text: *Poems* (c. 1929–1940), MS 3215, National Library of Ireland, where it is dated 1929.

Title: in Ovid's *Metamorphoses*, Pygmalion is a sculptor who makes a statue representing his ideal of womanhood and falls in love with his own creation; Venus, the goddess of love, brings it to life in answer to his prayer.

Roscommon is a county in Ireland; Ballahedreen is a phonetic spelling of Ballaghaderreen in the neighbouring county of Mayo; Boyle is a town in County Roscommon.

In a second manuscript version (MS 9579, National Library of Ireland) l. 12 is 'Once lifted to a grey terrific smile'.

Ploughman

First publication: the *Irish Statesman* (15 February 1930).

Source text: *Ploughman and Other Poems* (1936).

'Ploughman', 'The Intangible' and 'Dreamer', printed in the *Irish Statesman*, were the first poems of Kavanagh's accepted for publication by a literary journal. 'Ploughman' was included by Thomas Moult in *The Best Poems of 1930* (London, 1930).

In *The Green Fool* (1938, p. 219) Kavanagh writes that the origin of this 'ploughman ecstasy' was 'a kicking mare in a rusty old plough tilling a rood of land for turnips'.

After May
First publication: the *Irish Times* (15 June 1935).
Source text: *Ploughman and Other Poems* (1936).

Tinker's Wife
Source text: *Ploughman and Other Poems* (1936).

Inniskeen Road: July Evening
First publication and source text: *Ploughman and Other Poems* (1936).
The first published poem in which Kavanagh names people and places in his native parish of Inniskeen: there is a road called Inniskeen Road and 'Billy Brennan's barn' actually existed.
Alexander Selkirk (1676–1721), the model for Robinson Crusoe, was a Scottish sailor who quarrelled with the captain of his ship and at his own request was put ashore on the uninhabited island of Mas in the Juan Fernandez cluster. He remained there alone for over four years until he was discovered and rescued in February 1709. Kavanagh's sonnet alludes to the opening stanza of William Cowper's 'Verses supposed to be written by Alexander Selkirk' (1782), which begins, 'I am monarch of all I survey' and includes the lines

> Oh solitude! where are the charms
> That sages have seen in thy face?
> Better dwell in the midst of alarms,
> Than reign in this horrible place.

Sanctity
First publication: the *Dublin Magazine* (July/September 1936).
Source text: *A Soul for Sale* (1947).

The Hired Boy
First publication and source text: *Ireland Today* (October 1936).
The first poem in which Kavanagh rails against small-farm life.

John Maguire anticipates Patrick Maguire of *The Great Hunger*, which is also set in Donaghmoyne, a parish adjacent to Inniskeen which once formed part of Inniskeen parish.

'York pig' is a breed of pig.

Shancoduff

First publication: the *Dublin Magazine* (July/September 1937) as 'Shanco Dubh'.

Source text: *Come Dance with Kitty Stobling* (1960) where it was dated 1934.

This was Kavanagh's favourite early poem; it was much revised for republication in *Nimbus* (winter 1956).

Title: Reynolds' Farm, a small farm purchased by Kavanagh's father, was situated in the townland of Shancoduff. It is mentioned in *The Green Fool* (1938, p. 204), where the first stanza of the poem is quoted.

The hills are 'black', a translation of the Gaelic *dubh* (anglicized to 'duff'), because they are north-facing.

Armagh is a cathedral city; the diocese of Armagh is the see of the principal archbishop of the Catholic Church and Church of Ireland.

'Lot's wife' in the Old Testament (Genesis 19) was changed to a pillar of salt because of her curiosity; she looked back at the cities of Sodom and Gomorrah from whose destruction she and her husband had been saved. Kavanagh's 'parochial' aesthetic (see Introduction) advocated indifference to the metropolitan.

Glassdrummond, the Big Forth of Rocksavage and the Featherna Bush are local place-names. A 'forth' is a prehistoric hill-fort, a low mound, here playfully identified with the Matterhorn in Switzerland, the highest peak in the Alps.

The 'cattle-drovers' are dealers, buying and selling the cattle the farmer nurtures; 'them . . . hills' mimics their vernacular speech.

Poplar Memory

First publication: *The Complete Poems* (1972).

Source text: *The Seed and the Soil* (1937). Unpublished collection (MS 9579, National Library of Ireland).

'From' in l. 4 has been substituted for the manuscript version 'For'.

Plough-Horses

First publication and source text: *Fifty Years of Modern Verse*, ed. John Gawsworth (London, 1938).

Phidias, active about 475–430 BC, was a Greek sculptor whose statuary was idealized and characterized by quiet stances and serene expressions.

Snail

First publication: *The Complete Poems* (1972).

Source text: *To Anna Quinn* (1938). Unpublished collection (MS 9579, National Library of Ireland).

Memory of My Father

First publication: the *Dublin Magazine* (October/December 1939).

Source text: *A Soul for Sale* (1947).

Kavanagh's father had died on 27 August 1929.

Gardiner (pronounced 'Gardner') Street is in Dublin.

To the Man After the Harrow

First publication: the *Irish Times* (6 April 1940).

Source text: *Come Dance with Kitty Stobling* (1960) where it was dated 1936.

The 'Hebrew Book' is the Bible.

Brady is a common local surname, also used in *Tarry Flynn* (1948).

In the Old Testament (Genesis 1), 'the earth was without form and void; and darkness was upon the face of the deep', until God said, 'Let there be light.' Mist or fog is a favourite metaphor of Kavanagh's to signify the pre-conscious state in which poetry is gestated – cf. 'Kerr's Ass'.

The worm's opinion of harrowing may allude to Rudyard Kipling's lines in *Departmental Ditties* (1886):

The toad beneath the harrow knows
Exactly where each tooth point goes.
The butterfly upon the road
Preaches contentment to that toad.

Spraying the Potatoes

First publication: the *Irish Times* (27 July 1940).

Source text: *A Soul for Sale* (1947).

Title: potato-plants (of which 'Kerr's Pinks' and 'Arran Banners' are two varieties) were sprayed with a chemical to prevent disease or 'blight'; the farmer walked along each row (drill) of plants with a two-gallon sprayer strapped to his back, refilling it from a large barrel of the toxic substance. Copper sulphate was a chemical used, hence 'copper-poisoned'.

In the Book of Ruth in the Old Testament, Ruth is a young exiled widow who marries Boaz, an older man in whose barley field she works.

Stony Grey Soil

First publication: the *Bell* (October 1940). The first number of this journal.

Source text: *A Soul for Sale* (1947).

When first published, the poem was dedicated to Sean O'Faolain, then a friend as well as founding editor of the *Bell*. It was paired with a celebratory poem, 'Kednaminsha', in which a local place was personified and apostrophized. (Kavanagh attended primary school in Kednaminsha.)

'weasel itch'. An irritation of the skin caused by wearing clothes with which the animal has been in contact.

'swinish food'. The allusion may be to Circe in Homer's *Odyssey* who metamorphosed Ulysses' sailors into pigs.

Mullahinsha, Drummeril and Black Shanco (Shancoduff) are Inniskeen place-names.

A Christmas Childhood

First publication: part I in the *Irish Press* (24 December 1943); part II in the *Bell* (December 1940).

Source text: *A Soul for Sale* (1947).

Lennon, Callan and Cassidy are common local surnames – cf. 'Art McCooey', 'Threshing Morning' and 'Literary Adventures'.

Cassiopeia is a northern constellation clearly visible from Ireland.

Art McCooey

First publication: the *Bell* (April 1941).

Source text: *A Soul for Sale* (1947).

Title: Art McCooey was an eighteenth-century Gaelic poet from a small-farm background who lived in Creggan, a district near Inniskeen, and occasionally worked as a farm labourer. Folklore tells how he once became so absorbed in composing a poem that he drove the same cartful of manure between the manure-heap and the place where he was supposed to deposit his load, until he was caught in the act by his enraged employer and brought to his senses with a few rough words. Kavanagh's knowledge of Gaelic was rudimentary, but he felt an affection for the Gaelic-speaking poets of his own region, regarding them as 'rude fore-fathers' who had to some extent anticipated his own 'parochial' programme: '. . . though they were not great poets, they absorbed the little fields and lanes and became authentic through them' ('A Poet's Country', *Ireland of the Welcomes*, March 1953).

County Cavan borders on Kavanagh's home county, Monaghan, and was sometimes substituted for it as a fictional location, e.g. in *Tarry Flynn* (1948).

Inniskeen idiom is used for the characters' speech in this poem and, the title excepted, the personal names are typical local names; 'wangel' is a local dialect word for a handful of straw tied at one end.

The Long Garden

First publication: the *Listener* (11 December 1941).

Source text: *A Soul for Sale* (1947).

This is an excerpt from a long, unpublished poem, 'Why Sorrow?', presented as an independent lyric. (For 'Why Sorrow?' see note on

'Father Mat'. In 'Why Sorrow?' the lyric was written in the third
person and described the childhood of an old poet-priest, Father
Mat; it was changed to the first person for journal publication.

In Greek mythology a tree bearing golden apples was guarded by
the Hesperides, the daughters of evening, who lived in the west
beyond the sunset.

Carrick is Carrickmacross in County Monaghan, the nearest town to
Inniskeen; Candle-Fort and Drumcatton are local place-names.

The Great Hunger

First publication: parts I, II, III and twenty-six lines from part IV
under the title 'The Old Peasant' in *Horizon*, vol. 5, no. 25
(January 1942), with a note that this 'is a long poem of 30 pages
of which only the beginning is . . . given'. The complete poem,
with parts I, II, III revised and part IV substantially changed,
was published by the Cuala Press, Dublin, in April 1942. A
version, omitting ll. 9–32 of part II, but otherwise only slightly
revised, was the concluding poem in *A Soul for Sale* (1947).
When Kavanagh made a holograph copy of *The Great Hunger*
for the National Library of Ireland, he inserted a note that the
poem was completed in October 1941. *The Great Hunger* was out
of print until it appeared in *Collected Poems* (1964).

Source text: *The Great Hunger*, the Cuala Press, Dublin, April 1942.

Censorship and bowdlerization: the edition of *Horizon* in which
part of *The Great Hunger* first appeared was an 'Irish number'
which was seized by the Irish police. Their interest in this Eng-
lish monthly may have been connected with state censorship of
information about Irish affairs during the Second World War.
Though the police visited and questioned Kavanagh, their atti-
tude was friendly and unthreatening.

Surprisingly, the Cuala Press edition of *The Great Hunger* es-
caped being banned in Ireland on grounds of indecency under
the Censorship of Publications Act of 1929, despite the references
to masturbation in parts II, V and VIII, and the numerous
explicit sexual allusions throughout. (Kate O'Brien's novel *The*

Land of Spices had been banned in 1941 because it contained one decorous allusion to a homosexual affair.) The censors' oversight on this occasion may probably be attributed to the fact that *The Great Hunger* was a poem, and that it appeared in a limited edition of 250 copies.

The bowdlerization of twenty-nine lines from part II of the *A Soul for Sale* edition was done at Kavanagh's suggestion because he thought they were 'perhaps too obscene' (letter dated 6 October 1945 in the Macmillan Archive, the British Library). He asked the editors of *Collected Poems* to return to the unexpurgated Cuala Press version (Martin Green, letter to *The Times Literary Supplement*, 26 August–1 September 1988).

Title: the Great Hunger is a synonym for the great famine in Ireland in the mid nineteenth century (see Introduction). Cecil Woodham-Smith published a book about the Irish famine under this title in 1962 (republished by Penguin Books, Harmondsworth, 1991).

[I]

The opening line which perverts the biblical description of the conception and birth of Jesus Christ, 'And the Word was made flesh and dwelt amongst us' (St John 1:14), introduces a central theme of the poem, that Christianity has yielded to materialism in rural Ireland.

'the queen / Too long virgin' is probably an allusion to the Virgin Mary, whose virginity was invoked by the Catholic Church as a model of pre-marital chastity. The hymn beginning 'Hail Queen of Heaven, the ocean star' was very popular in Ireland and is quoted from in *The Green Fool* (1938, p. 29).

'apples . . . hung from the ceilings'. One of the games traditionally played at Hallowe'en (31 October) was to attempt the feat of biting an apple hung from the ceiling with one's arms tied behind one's back.

'heeled-up cart'. A cart resting on its tail-board with its shafts in the air.

'spanging'. A dialect word meaning 'leaping or moving rapidly'.

'ruckety'. A dialect word meaning 'uneven, not level'.

'clay-wattled moustache'. Possibly an ironic allusion to the would-be country-dweller in Yeats's 'The Lake Isle of Innisfree' (1906) who 'would build a hut there, of clay and wattles made'.

'a wet sack flapping about the knees'. Farm workers sometimes wore a sack, apron-fashion, over their trousers when kneeling in wet fields.

'The horse lifts its head and crashes'. 'Cranes' was substituted for 'crashes' in *A Soul for Sale* to achieve a half-rhyme with 'stones'.

'sole-plate'. Horseshoe.

Donaghmoyne. See note on 'The Hired Boy' above.

[III]

'whirring noise'. 'Stone' is substituted for 'noise' in *A Soul for Sale* to rhyme with 'alone'.

'Hop back . . . wae'. Maguire's instructions to his horse; 'Woa' means 'slow down' or 'stop'.

'prostitute's'. The use of the possessive case here is puzzling, but it remains unchanged in *A Soul for Sale*.

'Respectability that knows the price of all things'. An ironic allusion to the definition of a cynic in Oscar Wilde's play *Lady Windermere's Fan* (1892) as 'a man who knows the price of everything and the value of nothing'.

[IV]

'Maguire knelt . . . death'. Maguire is attending Mass. He absent-mindedly confuses phrases from two prayers: an invocation to Jesus, Mary and Joseph ('Jesus, Mary and Joseph, assist me in my last agony / Jesus, Mary and Joseph may I breathe forth my soul in peace with you. Amen') and the Hail Mary ('Pray for us now and at the hour of our death. Amen'). The phrases from both prayers focus on death, so though Maguire avoids the word he is shown to be obsessed with death.

'pregnant Tabernacle'. The shrine on the altar in which a conse-
crated host is kept is described as pregnant because, according
to Catholic belief, it houses the body of Christ.

'Maguire ... Amen'. He leaves before the Mass is quite over,
blessing himself at the holy water font in the church porch.

'Tree of Life'. This tree grew in the midst of the Garden of Eden
(Genesis 2:9).

[V]

'the cross-roads'. Country men used to gather at a local crossroads
in the evening to chat or to play a game of pitch and toss.

'Health ... compounds of'. Catholicism and pagan superstition
intermingle as the theological virtues of faith, hope and charity
are associated with fairies and with the three-wishes motif from
folklore.

[VI]

'and labelled like a case in a railway store'. This phrase was omitted
in *A Soul for Sale*, a printer's error, it would seem, since a space
has been left on the page. Subsequent editions (except the Irish
University Press facsimile edition of 1971) have continued to
omit the phrase, though to do so makes a nonsense of the
sentence.

'In a crumb of bread'. This alludes to the Catholic doctrine that a
wafer of unleavened bread is transubstantiated into the body of
Christ during Mass.

'three wishes were three stones'. In folklore and fairytale those who
are granted three wishes are generally cheated of what they desire.

[IX]

'silver bowl of knowledge'. William Blake was one of Kavanagh's
favourite poets and this phrase may be based on some lines from
The Book of Thel (1789):

> Can Wisdom be put in a silver rod?
> Or Love in a golden bowl?

'low ceiling'. The country chapel customarily had a very high ceiling; Kavanagh deliberately lowers it to suggest the oppressiveness of rural Catholicism.

'Birds of Paradise'. This species is renowned for its colourful plumage.

'old book found in a king's tomb'. The allusion may be to Howard Carter's excavations in the Valley of the Kings in Egypt (Carter had died in 1939).

[X]

'*Reynolds' News* or the *Sunday Dispatch*'. Two popular newspapers.

'almanac'. *Old Moore's Almanac* was a book found in most Irish rural households.

'school reader'. Kavanagh had been heavily dependent on school readers for his own education. (See Introduction.)

'strainer'. A perforated household utensil similar to a sieve.

'a bob'. This was a shilling; five pence in decimal coinage.

'the Derby'. The name of an annual horse-race at the Epsom race-course in England.

'the Guineas'. The name of an annual horse-race at the Newmarket race-course in England.

'each way', 'double', 'treble', 'full multiple odds' are betting terms.

The war being discussed by Maguire and his neighbours is the First World War; the poem was written during the Second.

[XI]

'crookened'. A homely way of saying 'made crooked'.

'hold the collecting box'. It was a mark of trustworthiness to be assigned the task of collecting a voluntary cash contribution from parishioners on their way into Sunday Mass.

Mat Talbot (1856–1925) was a Dublin working man who was an

alcoholic until the age of twenty-eight, when he reformed and, thereafter, devoted his leisure time to prayer and penance. At his death it was discovered that he wore chains on his body. Talbot gave alms to the needy and was particularly friendly towards children; like Maguire, he lived with his mother until her death.

The references to card-playing are to the game of whist.

'tanner'. Sixpence in pre-decimal coinage.

[XII]

Brannagan's Gap was situated not far from the Kavanagh home in Inniskeen.

'buck-leaped'. Leaped about like a frisky animal. Kavanagh later coined the phrase 'the national bucklep' to refer to the antics of those profiteering from their Irishness in chauvinist, post-colonial Ireland.

'Champed'. Pounded. A national dish, 'champ', was made of pounded or mashed potatoes.

'Punch and Judy'. In this popular puppet-show, Punch and Judy were a grotesque married couple who quarrelled incessantly.

'crooks'. The mother's fingers are wasted and twisted with arthritis.

'the tick'. The mattress; ticking was the striped fabric in which a mattress was encased.

'the litany' and 'the holy water'. The deathbed rituals alluded to here, the recitation of the 'Litany for a Soul Departing' and the sprinkling of holy water, are more fully described in *The Green Fool* (1938, chapter 21).

'the procession'. A Catholic devotional practice in which a congregation walks in procession, saying prayers and/or singing hymns. Such processions take place in summer and are festive occasions.

[XIII]

The first two paragraphs are ironic about the cult of primitivism which was associated with the Literary and Gaelic Revivals in the years preceding Independence and was embraced by the Taoiseach Eamon De Valera in the early 1940s. (See Introduction.)

[XIV]

Lammas is 1 August.

'an oil-less lamp'. This sexual allusion is based on the fact that oil-lamps were common in rural Ireland; electricity was not switched on in Inniskeen until 17 December 1953.

'The hungry fiend'. The life-denying force in rural Ireland, described as diabolic because it is opposed to the life-giving God.

'the apocalypse of clay'. The poem begins and ends by announcing the ultimate triumph of 'clay', materialism, over the spiritual and the divine. The Apocalypse is the revelation of the future granted to St John in the Book of Revelation in the Bible.

'this land'. The plight of Maguire and his fellow-parishioners is representative of a nationwide disaster.

Lough Derg

First publication: posthumously collected in *November Haggard*, ed. Peter Kavanagh, New York, 1971. Simultaneously published in book form by Martin, Brian and O'Keeffe, London, and the Goldsmith Press, the Curragh (Ireland), in 1978.

Source text: typescript in the Kavanagh Archive, University College, Dublin (Kav/B/2). The only surviving typescript version, this includes many variants on previously published versions.

Kavanagh visited Lough Derg twice, in June 1940 and 1942. The poem was written soon after his 1942 pilgrimage; the address on the typescript is '9 Lr. O'Connell St, Dublin', to which Kavanagh moved on 30 June 1942.

Title: Lough Derg, an island off the coast of County Donegal in the Republic of Ireland, has been a place of penitential pilgrimage since the Middle Ages. Kavanagh's poem documents the pilgrimage quite faithfully, though he spares the reader many of its rigours. The pilgrimage is a gruelling physical ordeal. The barefoot pilgrims are expected to fast from the midnight prior to their arrival on the island; they must maintain an all-night vigil on their first night; their diet is black tea or coffee and dry toast or 'Lough Derg soup', hot water flavoured with salt and pepper. They spend much of their time performing 'stations' which include walking barefoot around or kneeling on rings of stones known as 'beds'. These 'beds' or penitential cells are the remains of beehive cells from the early monastic period and are named after Saints Brigid, Brendan, Catherine, Columba, Davog, Kevin, Molaise and Patrick. Pilgrims spend two nights on the island, arriving on the afternoon of the first day and leaving on the morning of the third.

Lough Derg as a topic has attracted many Irish writers. William Carleton, one of Kavanagh's Irish literary heroes, described the pilgrimage during the mid nineteenth century in his short story 'A Lough Derg Pilgrim' in *Traits and Stories of the Irish Peasantry* (1830–35). A realist literary account of the pilgrimage during the mid twentieth century is to be found in Sean O'Faolain's short story 'Lovers of the Lake' (*The Collected Stories of Sean O'Faolain*, vol. 2, London, 1981). Denis Devlin published a poem, 'Lough Derg', in 1946, which Kavanagh reviewed unenthusiastically; Seamus Heaney's 'Station Island' (1984) draws allusively on the Lough Derg theme and refers to Kavanagh's pilgrimage.

Cavan, Leitrim and Mayo are three of Ireland's twenty-six counties. County Fermanagh, which is in Northern Ireland, borders on County Donegal and is very near Lough Derg.

'St Patrick's Purgatory' is an alternative name for Lough Derg; St Patrick is the patron saint of Ireland.

'Hail glorious St Patrick' is the opening phrase of a popular hymn.

The rosary, a very popular prayer in Catholic Ireland, is frequently recited aloud in church or in the home.

Benediction is a Catholic service during which a monstrance containing the Host is held aloft by the priest; the monstrance is made of gold and the top part is circular and ornamented with rays so that it resembles popular pictorial representations of the sun.

'Holy, Holy, Holy, Lord God of Hosts' is the beginning of a liturgical prayer recited during Mass.

For 'procession', see note on *The Great Hunger*, part XII.

'Congresses'. A eucharistic congress that was held in Dublin for a week in June 1932 brought an unprecedented influx of Catholics to the Irish capital; it concluded with an open-air Mass in the Phoenix Park, attended by over a million people.

Muckno Street is in the town of Castleblaney in County Monaghan.

'St Brigid's Cross'. St Brigid, sometimes referred to as the Mary of the Gael, founded a famous Abbey at Kildare in the fifth or sixth century.

'Prior'. The priest who oversees the Lough Derg pilgrimages.

'Carrara . . . lost'. Irish religious statuary was sometimes made of marble from Carrara in Tuscany, Italy; an alb is a white liturgical vestment reaching to the feet. The shamrock, a three-leaved clover, is Ireland's national emblem; it is associated with St Patrick because he is said to have used it to explain the Christian mystery of the Trinity.

'agnisties' is the plural of a colloquial pronunciation of the Latin phrase *Agnus Dei*, literally 'lamb of God'. *Agnus Deis* were small wax or silken padded discs, stamped with the device of a lamb bearing a cross or flag; they were blessed by the Church and were treated as devotional objects by pious Catholics.

'Catholic Truth pamphlets'. The Catholic Truth Society of Ireland, founded in 1899, attempted to counter the spread of immoral literature by publishing and distributing popular, inexpensive, Catholic pamphlets and tracts.

For 'the Famine', see the notes on *The Great Hunger* above. As a consequence of the famine there was vast emigration overseas.

'Megrim' is a migraine, but also a whim or fancy.

The scene in 'John Flood's cottage' with its blend of sociability and solemnity resembles an Irish 'wake', a vigil kept by family

and neighbours over a corpse. For a description of 'waking' as
Kavanagh had known it, see *The Green Fool* (1938, pp. 165–6).

A 'Holy Biddy' (based on a common abbreviation of the common
female name Brigid) is a variant of the more customary expres-
sion 'a Holy Mary', a derogatory term for a pious woman.
'Diddy' is a colloquialism for vagina.

'pursuing French-hot miracles' refers to pilgrimages to Lourdes in
the south-west of France, where the Blessed Virgin Mary is
reputed to have appeared in 1858 to a peasant girl, Bernadette
Soubirous. The waters of a spring, which marks the spot where
the Virgin appeared, are believed to have miraculous healing
powers. The Lourdes pilgrimage is still popular with Irish
Catholics.

St Patrick's College, Maynooth, County Kildare, is Ireland's prin-
cipal seminary for the education of priests. It is now also a
constituent college of the National University of Ireland.

'music-hall tunes'. In *The Green Fool* (p. 16), Kavanagh's father
sings these lines from 'A Starry Night':

> A starry night for a ramble
> Through the flowery dell
> Beneath the bush and bramble
> Kiss but never tell . . .

Roscommon. See note on 'Pygmalion' above.

'Hail Queen of Heaven'. See note on *The Great Hunger*, part I,
above.

'The Apostles' Creed' is a profession of Christian faith and it is the
prayer with which the rosary begins; here there is no separation
between the sacred and the secular. Christianity seems so recent
and so local to the pilgrims that Christ is like some deceased
notoriety, still remembered by one of their neighbours.

'the dying sparrow'. 'Are not five sparrows sold for two farthings,
and not one of them is forgotten before God?' (St Luke 12:6).

'the middle of a war'. The Second World War was in progress
when this poem was written.

The 'Communion of Saints' is the fellowship of all Christians living and dead.

A 'caravan' here refers to a Middle Eastern company of merchants or pilgrims travelling together for safety.

AOH is the Ancient Order of Hibernians, a Catholic counter-organization to the Protestant Orange Order, founded *c.*1838, but unified and strengthened in the early twentieth century. It supported John Redmond (1856–1918), chairman of the Irish parliamentary party in the British House of Commons from 1900, who promoted the achievement of Home Rule for Ireland by constitutional means.

Ireland 'froze for want of Europe' because its policy of neutrality during the Second World War isolated it from the rest of Europe.

Rathfriarland is probably Rathfriland in County Down, Northern Ireland; Derry or Londonderry is a city and county in Northern Ireland; Wicklow is a town and county and Kerry a county in what is now the Republic of Ireland.

'Our Lady of Miraculous Succour'. 'Our Lady of Perpetual Succour' is the usual title. A litany is a prayer consisting of a series of petitions or apostrophes, each responded to by a repeated formula. The correct formula here is 'We beseech thee to hear us' but the woman slurs it slightly.

'Intermediate'. The Intermediate Certificate was a public examination which pupils sat after two or three years in a secondary school. It has since been replaced.

The sonnet to St Anne is based on the once-popular jingle 'O good St Anne / Send me a man / As fast as you can'.

'Dempsey . . . Tunney'. Jack Dempsey (1895–1983) was world heavyweight boxing champion from 1919 to 1926, when he lost his title to Gene Tunney (1897–1978). He lost to Tunney again in 1927, and this bout, known as 'the battle of the Long Count', was one of the most controversial in boxing history. Dempsey did not retire from the ring until 1940.

Cornelius Jansen (1585–1638) inspired the religious revival known

as Jansenism, an attempt to reform the Church of Rome. Many
of his own teachings and those of his followers were pronounced
heretical. In Ireland, Jansenism is popularly associated with
sexual repression and is thought to have influenced priests edu-
cated in Maynooth. In 'Sex and Christianity' (*Kavanagh's Weekly*,
24 May 1952), Kavanagh remarks that 'somewhere in the 19th
century' Ireland became infected with 'an anti-life heresy' dis-
seminated by priests trained in Maynooth.

Rostov on the River Don in southern Russia was the scene of fierce
fighting during the war; it was under attack by Germany in
June 1942 and was captured at the end of July.

Pettigo is a town that straddles the border between Northern
Ireland and what is now the Republic of Ireland; half of it is in
County Donegal and half in County Fermanagh; Dundalk, Bun-
doran and Omagh are towns in Counties Louth, Donegal and
Tyrone respectively.

Advent

First publication: the *Irish Times* (24 December 1942) as
'Renewal'.

Source text: *A Soul for Sale* (1947).

Title: Advent is the ecclesiastical term for the season leading up to
the feast of the Nativity; it includes the four Sundays immedi-
ately preceding Christmas Day. Here it coincides with a season
of aesthetic asceticism that will purge the poet of worldly
sophistication.

'Time begins' because the birth of Christ occurred in AD 1 and
because each Christmas is followed by a new year.

The poem consists of two sonnets; the second was originally divided
into two stanzas, like the first.

Consider the Grass Growing

First publication and source text: the *Irish Press* (21 May 1943).
Untitled.

This, and part of the following poem, were among the snippets of verse which Kavanagh included in the twice-weekly 'City Commentary' column which he contributed to the daily newspaper the *Irish Press* between September 1942 and February 1944 under the pseudonym Piers Plowman.

Peace

Source text: *Come Dance with Kitty Stobling* (1960), where it is dated 1943 (Dublin).

Britain declared war on Germany on 3 September 1939, a few weeks after Kavanagh took up residence in Dublin, so 'childhood country' is associated with peace and Dublin with a fight against tyrants.

Threshing Morning

First publication: a variant version of the first three stanzas, entitled 'A Reverie of Poor Piers', in Kavanagh's 'City Commentary' column, the *Irish Press* (27 September 1943). (A variant version of the remainder of the poem, entitled 'Threshing Morning', is included in a holograph collection of poems *c.*1929–40, MS 3215, in the National Library of Ireland. The page containing the three stanzas was possibly removed for use in the *Irish Press*.) The entire poem was printed in the novel *Tarry Flynn* (1948, pp. 188–9) and it also includes a variant version of the fourth stanza (p. 91).

Source text: *Tarry Flynn* (1948). Untitled.

In *Tarry Flynn*, which concludes with this poem, it is attributed to the eponymous hero, a farmer-poet.

The personal names Cassidy and Mary are used in the novel: Eusebius Cassidy is, ostensibly, Tarry's friend; Mary Reilly, the daughter of a prosperous local farmer, is the woman with whom he is in love.

'Chaffy' puns on 'husks of corn' and 'banter'.

A Wreath for Tom Moore's Statue

First publication: the *Irish Times* (4 March 1944) as 'Statue, Symbol and Poet'.

Source text: *A Soul for Sale* (1947).

Title: the original title was followed by the disclaimer 'Not concerning Thomas Moore'.

Thomas Moore (1779–1852) is best known for his *Irish Melodies* (1807–34), a series of lyrics based on traditional Irish airs. His status in the nineteenth century was almost that of Irish national bard. However, Moore's statue, which stands beside Trinity College, Dublin, and dates from October 1857, has been described by his biographer as 'a libel in metal, holding him up to posterity's ridicule and contempt' (Terence de Vere White, *Tom Moore*, London, 1977, p. xii).

'An old shopkeeper'. Kavanagh seems to have been unaware that Moore's father was a Dublin grocer and that the poet was born and reared over the shop in Aungier Street.

'the vermin . . . exile's way'. The allusion is to Stephen Dedalus's comment on the statue in Joyce's *A Portrait of the Artist as a Young Man* (1916) that 'sloth of the body and of the soul crept over it like unseen vermin'.

Pegasus

First publication: the *Irish Times* (1 July 1944) as 'A Glut on the Market'.

Source text: *A Soul for Sale* (1947), where it was the opening poem.

Title: winged horse that caused the spring of Hippocrene to flow on Mt. Helicon, home of the Muses, hence fig. poetic genius.

Kavanagh was without regular weekly employment from February 1944 to February 1946 and the poem expresses his bitterness at his inability to earn a livelihood in Ireland. Cyril Connolly remarked on the precarious financial position of the Irish writer in the January 1942 issue of *Horizon*: '. . . a population of three and a half millions cannot support very many intellectuals, and this generates something of the famous Dublin bitterness'.

Selling one's soul to the devil for a rich reward was a well-established motif in literature (the Faust theme) and in Irish folklore. Kavanagh later dismissed the poem as 'a terrible piece', a 'dissolute character whining', but said his 'English publishers loved it' (*Studies*, spring 1959).

Memory of Brother Michael

First publication: the *Irish Times* (14 October 1944).

Source text: *A Soul for Sale* (1947).

Title: Brother Michael (1575–*c*.1645), a Franciscan monk, was an historian who, between 1632 and 1636, compiled with the aid of three other historians *Annala Rioghachta Eireann* (Annals of the Kingdom of Ireland), commonly known as *The Annals of the Four Masters*. The *Annals* are mostly a chronicle of facts and dates, recording the history of Ireland to 1616. Brother Michael's historiography was important because it preserved information which might otherwise have been lost with the destruction of manuscripts and the suppression of the old Gaelic order after the Cromwellian plantations.

This poem was a favourite with anthologists, but Kavanagh later repudiated it both because it was 'bad history' and because of 'how appallingly' it accepted 'the myth of Ireland as a spiritual entity' (*Studies*, spring 1959).

Shakespeare, Marlowe, Jonson, Drake. Kavanagh, who was scornful about Ireland's obsession with its own history, compares Ireland's past unfavourably with England's.

Brendan was a sixth-century Irish saint who was the hero of an eighth-century Latin prose masterpiece *Navigatio Brendani* (The Voyage of St Brendan), a tale of adventures at sea which includes the saint's voyage to America.

Bluebells for Love

First publication: the *Bell* (June 1945) as 'Bluebells'.

Source text: *A Soul for Sale* (1947).

'big trees'. Originally 'beech trees'.

Dunshaughlin is a small town in County Meath.

Temptation in Harvest

First publication: the first three sonnets of the sequence, with some variants, were published in the *Irish Times* (1 September 1945) as 'The Monaghan Accent', with a note that this was a 'fragment from a sequence'. The final two sonnets, with some variants, appeared in the *Irish Times* (29 June 1946), under the present title; an accompanying note indicates that they are the end of a sequence.

Source text: *A Soul for Sale* (1947).

Title: the conflict between the claims of his native countryside and his artistic vocation is a recurring theme in Kavanagh's writings. As late as *Self-Portrait* (1964), he was still puzzling over his self-imposed exile from Inniskeen in 1939. The lure of the artistic life is personified as a diabolic tempter in 'Father Mat', and in *Tarry Flynn* (1948) Tarry's uncle is a human tempter who persuades Tarry to leave home; both texts were being revised at approximately the same time as the writing of 'Temptation in Harvest'. So ambivalent is the attitude to both country and city in this sonnet sequence that returning to the farm or quitting it are both represented as temptations.

Sonnet 3. Drummeril is an Inniskeen place-name, also used in 'Stony Grey Soil'.

Sonnet 4. Parnassus. See note on 'Intimate Parnassus' below.

'Christ in Gethsamane'. Christ's agony in Gethsamane is recorded in St Matthew 26 and St Mark 14.

Sonnet 5. 'Egypt . . . City of the Kings'. In a metaphor based on the Book of Exodus in the Old Testament, Dublin is represented as Jerusalem and the country poet as an exiled Israelite reluctant to leave his enslavement in Egypt. 'Flaggers' are wild irises which grow on marshy ground.

Sonnet 6. The biblical metaphor is sustained by the allusion to the burning bush in which God appeared to Moses in Exodus 3.

Father Mat

First publication: the first two stanzas, untitled, in the *Standard*

(5 October 1945); the last three stanzas of part II and all of part III were printed as a continuous poem, entitled 'Through the Open Door . . .' in *Irish Writing*, no.1 (October 1946), followed by a note: 'The above lines are taken from a poem Father Mat.'
Source text: *A Soul for Sale* (1947).

'Father Mat' is a much abbreviated and revised version of a long, unfinished and unpublished poem, 'Why Sorrow?' (Kav/B/40, Kavanagh Archive, University College, Dublin). The original poem, which included a lengthy flashback on Father Mat's life-history, focused on his vocational crisis: he was torn between his responsibility towards his dependent and trusting parishioners and his attraction towards paganism and poetry. The revised poem is more self-consciously 'parochial' and Father Mat's temptation to leave the priesthood is downplayed.

[I]

'May Devotions'. An evening service in the church throughout May in honour of the Virgin Mary.

The Christian Brothers are a religious congregation founded by Edmund Ignatius Rice (1762–1844) in Waterford, Ireland, in 1802 to teach poor Catholic boys.

In Memory of My Mother

First publication: the *Standard* (7 December 1945).
Source text: *Come Dance with Kitty Stobling* (1960).
Kavanagh's mother, Bridget Kavanagh, died in her seventy-third year on 10 November 1945.

On Raglan Road

First publication: the *Irish Press* (3 October 1946) as 'Dark Haired Miriam Ran Away'.
Source text: *Collected Poems* (1964).
Title: Raglan Road in Dublin is very close to Pembroke Road where Kavanagh lived from 1946 to 1958. He moved to 19 Raglan Road in 1958 and lived there until 1959.

Grafton Street is a fashionable Dublin street.

No Social Conscience

First publication and source text: the *Irish Times* (15 January 1949) as 'The Hero'. The title changed in *Collected Poems* (1964) which omitted the fourth stanza.

Title: Kavanagh pronounced a 'social conscience' to be the 'most hypocritical of appendages' for a poet: 'The poet may be human and humane, but he is not humanitarian, which is another way of saying that he isn't a fraud' (*Envoy*, June 1950).

'Emergency'. A word current in neutral Ireland to refer to the Second World War; Kavanagh and many others objected to this usage because it downplayed the seriousness of the war.

The Paddiad

First publication: *Horizon* (August 1949).

Source text: *Come Dance with Kitty Stobling* (1960) where the poem is preceded by the following 'Note':

> This satire is based on the sad notion with which my youth was infected that Ireland was a spiritual entity. I had a good deal to do with putting an end to this foolishness, for as soon as I found out I reported the news widely. It is now only propagated by the BBC in England and in the Bronx in New York and the departments of Irish literature at Princeton, Yale, Harvard and New York universities.
>
> I have included this satire but wish to warn the reader that it is based on the above-mentioned false and ridiculous premises.

Title: 'The Paddiad' is loosely modelled on *The Dunciad* (1743) by Alexander Pope; Pope's literary dunces are replaced by literary Paddies, and a Dublin pub is substituted for Grub Street.

Stanza 1. Kavanagh hinted that the location was the Pearl Bar, a contemporary haunt of Dublin's literati, when he wrote in *Poetry* (Chicago), in August 1949, that there was a good deal of 'low literary life' in Dublin, particularly in the Pearl Bar with 'Paddy Drunk and Paddy Sober / Slobbering over their pints of porter'. The Pearl Bar, which was opposite the *Irish Times* offices on Fleet Street, no longer exists.

Kavanagh privately identified the Paddies: 'Paddy of the Celtic Mist – Austin Clarke and other personalities; Chestertonian Paddy Frog – Robert Farren; in their middle sits a fellow – Maurice Walsh and other personalities' (Kav/B/80, Kavanagh Archive, University College, Dublin). 'Chestertonian' alludes to the corpulent English writer G. K. Chesterton (1874–1936). Since Chesterton was a brilliant and ebullient conversationalist and a versatile and witty writer, the allusion is misplaced.

W. B. Yeats had died in January 1939.

Stanza 2. 'a fellow'. Maurice Walsh (1879–1964) was a Kerry-born best-selling novelist whose fictions were mostly set in Scotland or in a romanticized West of Ireland. The popular Hollywood film *The Quiet Man* was based on one of his stories.

Mediocrity was one of Kavanagh's favourite terms of abuse; here it is personified as Lucifer, but it also corresponds to Pope's goddess, Dullness.

Lucifer was the name given to the chief rebel angel, Satan, in the Old Testament (Isaiah 14:12); his sin against God was motivated by pride.

Stanza 5. Sir Alfred James Munnings (1878–1959) was an English painter who specialized in the painting of horses. President of the Royal Academy, 1944–49, he was an outspoken opponent of modern art. For Pegasus, see note on Kavanagh's poem 'Pegasus' above.

Stanza 6. The Medici, a wealthy and influential Florentine family who flourished during the Renaissance, are remembered as exceptionally generous and enlightened patrons of the arts.

Stanza 7. 'A great renaissance' refers back to the European Renaissance in the previous stanza, but also to the period known as the Irish Literary Renaissance or Revival (*c.* 1880–1930).

Paddy Conscience was identified by Kavanagh as 'the author among others' (Kav/B/80). In his role of Ireland's literary conscience, the author identifies with Joyce, Yeats and Sean O'Casey. Stephen Dedalus in Joyce's *A Portrait of the Artist as a Young Man* (1916) went into exile to escape entrapment in the nets of 'nationality, language, religion' (p. 203). Yeats had satirized the Irish Catholic middle class, particularly in *Responsibilities* (1914). The dramatist Sean O'Casey went into permanent exile in England after the Abbey had rejected his play *The Silver Tassie* in 1928; a volume of his autobiography entitled *Inishfallen, Fare Thee Well* was published in 1949.

Stanza 9. Paddy Mist. Despite Kavanagh's claim that Paddy Mist is based on Austin Clarke, the similarities are not striking. Clarke (1896–1974) was a meticulous craftsman who adapted techniques from Gaelic verse to create an ethnic style in his poetry. Paddy Frog: Robert Farren/Roibeard O'Farachain (1909–84) was a poet, dramatist, critic, talks officer for Radio Eireann and, later, Controller of Programmes. He co-founded the Irish Lyric Theatre with Austin Clarke in 1944 and was a director of the Abbey Theatre 1940–73. Kavanagh's hostility towards Clarke and Farren was based on their promotion of an ethnic aesthetic (see Introduction). His review of Farren's *The Course of Irish Verse* (1948) was so savage that the *Irish Times* declined to publish it. The magnanimous Farren was largely responsible for the unbanning of *Tarry Flynn* in 1948.

A glass of plain is a half-pint of porter: the devil is a moderate drinker.

Stanza 10. Clare and Roscommon are two neighbouring Irish counties. (See Introduction for Kavanagh's views on 'parochialism'.)

Stanza 11. Connemara is a region near Galway city where Gaelic is spoken.

Stanza 13. James Stephens (1882–1950) wrote poetry and fiction. Though he is best known as the author of the novel *The Crock of Gold* (1912), he is probably included here because of his adaptations of Gaelic poetry.

Stanza 14. Kavanagh projected himself as an Olympian (see note on 'Freedom' below).

'Mummers' rantings'. This alludes to Joyce's self-dissociation from the Literary Revival in 'The Holy Office' (1927) where, parodying the opening lines of Yeats's 'To the Rose upon the Rood of Time' (1893), he wrote, 'But I must not accounted be / One of that mumming company.'

Stanza 15. The Irish author 'Dead in Paris' is not a specific reference.

Spring Day

First publication and source text: *Envoy* (March 1950). Untitled.

'Come all ye . . .' is a common opening phrase in Irish ballads.

W. B. refers, of course, to Yeats.

Stephen's Green is a park near the centre of Dublin city; Trinity College is close by; in 1950 University College was also close by, in Earlsfort Terrace.

Alfred Charles Kinsey (1894–1956). A North American zoologist who made an extensive and controversial study of the sexual life of humans. His two books, *Sexual Behaviour in the Human Male* (1948, the so-called 'Kinsey Report') and *Sexual Behaviour in the Human Female* (1953), were based on 18,500 personal interviews.

Kavanagh thought that this ballad was 'not a complete success', but that balladry should not be overlooked by poets: 'There is health in the barbaric simplicity of the ballad; it compels one to say something. Most of the verse written in this land suffers from one thing – it has nothing to say. Having something to say is largely a mood' (*Envoy*, March 1950).

Ante-Natal Dream

First publication: *Envoy* (July 1950).

Source text: *Come Dance with Kitty Stobling* (1960).

Title: as in 'Art McCooey', the young countryman is the future poet in a pre-natal stage, registering the sights and sounds of the countryside. His situation recalls the best known of Swift's images, that of Gulliver in Lilliput, a giant asleep on the ground surrounded by importunate pygmies.

Hayseed takes on metaphorical overtones: this seed will yield a literary crop.

Bank Holiday

First publication and source text: *Envoy* (September 1950) as 'Testament'. The title was changed to 'Bank Holiday' in *Collected Poems* (1964).

'the Waterloo and Searson's are two public-houses on Pembroke Road, Dublin, which Kavanagh would have passed on his daily walk into town from his apartment at 62 Pembroke Road.

l. 18. *Envoy* has 'them' instead of 'him', a misprint corrected in *Collected Poems* (1964).

Irish Poets Open Your Eyes

First publication and source text: *Envoy* (September 1950). Untitled.

In Kavanagh's *Envoy* 'Diary' this poem is prefaced by the comment: 'A new version of Yeats's poem is called for.' The poem is a rewriting of the penultimate section of Yeats's 'Under Ben Bulben' (1939) which begins, 'Irish poets learn your trade'.

Cabra is a working-class district in Dublin.

There is a greyhound race-track at Shelbourne Park in Dublin.

The 'Pro-Cathedral' is Dublin's principal Catholic church.

To Be Dead

First publication: *Envoy* (October 1950). Untitled.

Source text: *Come Dance with Kitty Stobling* (1960).

'perhaps' in l. 13 was omitted in *Envoy*.

Kerr's Ass

First publication: *Envoy* (October 1950). Untitled. Republished under the present title in the *Bell* (September 1953).

Source text: *Come Dance with Kitty Stobling* (1960).

The poem was first quoted in Kavanagh's *Envoy* 'Diary' where he argued that the speed of air travel had rendered the term exile 'melodramatic'. In the poem the sense of exile is comically displaced on to the ass.

'We borrowed the loan' is a colloquial tautology.

Dundalk is a prosperous market town in County Louth, about nine miles from Inniskeen; Mucker is the townland in Inniskeen in which Kavanagh was born and reared. 'Naming' played a vital role in the creative process for Kavanagh – cf. 'The Hospital'. Parts of the ass's harness are named in ll. 7–9; and the names of local people, places and things are juxtaposed with the two English place-names of l. 11.

Fog or mist was one of Kavanagh's favourite analogies for the unconscious state in which poetry is gestated – cf. 'To the Man After the Harrow'.

Who Killed James Joyce?

First publication and source text: *Envoy* (April 1951).

Title: the poem is based on the nursery rhyme quatrain 'Who Killed Cock Robin?', which Byron had also parodied in 'John Keats' (1821), the first line reading, 'Who Killed John Keats?' James Joyce (1882–1941) was the Irish writer whom Kavanagh most admired; he frequently alluded to his name or to his work, nominated him as one of his three great literary 'parishioners' (see Introduction), and said that *Ulysses* (1922) was one of his three favourite books and that he had read it 'scores of times' (*Kavanagh's Weekly*, 28 June 1952). *Envoy*, April 1951, was a special Joyce number, commemorating the tenth anniversary of his death. Kavanagh mischievously chose this occasion to comment ironically on the burgeoning Joyce cult, particularly in academe.

William Robert (Bertie) Rodgers (1909–69), a poet and broadcaster, was a Presbyterian minister at Loughgall, County Armagh, from 1935 to 1946 when he resigned to take a post with the BBC Third Programme in London. He presented a series of broadcasts on Irish writers, including one on Joyce. These broadcasts took the form of a symposium by living writers on their predecessors in which Kavanagh, on occasion, participated. They are collected in W. R. Rodgers, *Irish Literary Portraits* (London, 1972).

All Souls' Church at Langham Place, London, is close to Broadcasting House.

Trinity College, Dublin, founded in 1592, is Ireland's oldest university.

Bloomsday, 16 June 1904, the day on which *Ulysses* is set, is celebrated annually in Dublin by visiting the places mentioned in the novel, including the Martello tower at Sandycove (now a Joyce museum) where the opening scene takes place and the 'cabby's shelter' where Leopold Bloom and Stephen Dedalus converse in the penultimate, Eumaeus episode. The cabman's shelter is under the Loop Line bridge, near Butt Bridge and just west of the Custom House, on the northside of Dublin.

Though the Joyce cult is mocked in the poem, Kavanagh himself made the Bloomsday 'pilgrimage'; a well-known photograph taken on Sandymount Strand on 16 June 1954 shows him celebrating the fiftieth anniversary of Bloomsday with four friends including Brian O'Nolan (better known as Flann O'Brien).

Auditors In

First publication: the *Bell* (October 1951). Subtitled 'Speculations on a Theme'.

Source text: *Come Dance with Kitty Stobling* (1960).

Title: a pun on accountants/listeners: the account of the poet's assets and liabilities is conducted in a confessional mode.

[1]

Stanza 3. Gregory Rasputin (1871–1916), a Russian monk, enjoyed immense popularity and the reputation of a holy man among the peasants, and some of the nobility, including the imperial family. He demanded that his followers be united with him in soul and body, and his dictum 'sin in order that you may obtain forgiveness' resulted in wild orgies. The comparison with the Irish poet's situation is semi-ironic, since he depicts himself as too moralistic or idealistic to take advantage of his sex-appeal.

However, the Romantic association between the roles of poet and priest appealed to Kavanagh, who had made the connection as early as 'Why Sorrow?' (*c*.1941). For another comic treatment of this theme, see 'Cyrano de Bergerac'.

Stanza 5. Ednamo is a townland in Inniskeen; Willie Hughes' refers to an actual house. Affection for wild flowers and weeds is a recurring theme – cf. 'Bluebells for Love', 'On Reading a Book on Common Wild Flowers' and 'Prelude'.

'Not mere memory but the Real'. Recollection may stimulate poetic inspiration but is not to be confused with it; poetry creates a new present-tense reality – cf. 'Kerr's Ass' and 'On Reading a Book on Common Wild Flowers'.

'dig and ditch your authentic land'. Farming is now a metaphor for poetic art.

Stanza 6. Pembroke Road. Kavanagh lived at 62 Pembroke Road from September 1943 to October 1958. The area is referred to as a jungle in the 1948 poem 'Jungle', but is acknowledged as one of the poet's favourite haunts in 'If Ever You Go To Dublin Town'. (1953).

[II]

Sonnet 1. l. 10. This line begins 'Or' in the source text, an obvious misprint.

Sonnet 2. 'Away . . . ignore her'. Alludes to two of Stephen Dedalus's diary entries in the concluding lines of *A Portrait of the Artist as a Young Man* (1916). The entry for April 16 begins: 'Away! Away!' and concludes: 'making ready to go, shaking the wings of their exultant and terrible youth'. The next entry, April 26, begins: 'Mother is putting my new secondhand clothes in order, she prays now, she says, that I may learn in my own life and away from home and friends what the heart is and what it feels.'

Connolly's corner is a sharp bend on the road near Inniskeen village; Annavackey is a local townland; Armagh refers to the county.

Sonnet 3. Instead of opting for actual exile from Ireland, like

Stephen Dedalus or Joyce, the poet here chooses imaginative liberation from his Dublin context. 'Barren anger' and 'self-pitying melodrama' were features of Kavanagh's Dublin satires from the mid-1940s through the early 1950s, and for this reason the satires are under-represented in the present collection.

Innocence

First publication: the *Bell* (November 1951).
Source text: *Collected Poems* (1964).
Big Forth. See note on 'Shancoduff' above.
'Indian Summer' was 'Italian Summer' in the *Bell*.

Epic

First publication: the *Bell* (November 1951).
Source text: *Come Dance with Kitty Stobling* (1960).
'blue cast-steel'. The local combatants were armed with agricultural implements, forks or spades.
The 'march' is the boundary.
'Munich bother'. A deflationary reference to the 'Munich crisis' in 1938 when a world war consequent on Hitler's annexation of Czechoslovakia was temporarily averted at a conference in Munich.
'most important' was corrected to 'more important' in *Collected Poems* (1964).
Ballyrush and Gortin are two townlands in the parish of Inniskeen.
For Kavanagh's views on the 'local', see the Introduction.

On Looking into E. V. Rieu's Homer

First publication: the *Bell* (November 1951).
Source text: *Come Dance with Kitty Stobling* (1960).
Title: a comic allusion to Keats's sonnet 'On First Looking into Chapman's Homer' (1816); E. V. Rieu (1887–1972) was editor of the Penguin Classics from 1944 to 1964; his translation of Homer's *Iliad* was first published in 1950.

Far Field Rock. A local landmark. The 'fabulous mountain' is Mount Olympus in Thessaly, which is the dwelling-place of the gods in the *Iliad*.

God in Woman

First publication and source text: the *Bell* (November 1951).

I Had a Future

First publication and source text: *Kavanagh's Weekly* (12 April 1952).

'Who' in l. 14 was 'How' in *Kavanagh's Weekly*, an obvious misprint.

On first taking up residence in Dublin in August 1939, Kavanagh lived with his brother, Peter, on Upper Drumcondra Road.

The poet John Betjeman (1906–84), who was press attaché at the British Embassy in Dublin in 1940, befriended Kavanagh.

Wet Evening in April

First publication and source text: *Kavanagh's Weekly* (19 April 1952).

A Ballad

First publication and source text: *Kavanagh's Weekly* (14 June 1952) under the initials K. H.

Baggot Street in Dublin is a continuation of Pembroke Road, where Kavanagh resided at this date.

For Kavanagh's views on balladry, see note on 'Spring Day' above.

Having Confessed

First publication: *Kavanagh's Weekly* (5 July 1952). Untitled.

Source text: *Collected Poems* (1964).

The thirteenth and final number of *Kavanagh's Weekly* was devoted to a lengthy editorial which concluded with this poem, the first line of which originally read: 'Yet, having said all this he feels'.

'Lucifer'. See note on 'The Paddiad' above.

If Ever You Go To Dublin Town

First publication: the *Irish Times* (21 March 1953).

Source text: *Come Dance with Kitty Stobling* (1960).

Kavanagh customarily walked to the city centre from his Pembroke Road apartment via Baggot Street, the most direct route.

After Forty Years of Age

Source text: *Collected Poems* (1964).

I have been unable to trace the first publication of this poem. I presume it dates from the early 1950s because Kavanagh, as a late starter in literature, was prone to lie about his age, generally lopping off four years.

The Rowley Mile

First publication and source text: the *Bell* (January 1954).

This and 'Cyrano de Bergerac' were published together as 'Two Sentimental Songs'. The two poems are thematically and formally paired: both treat the subject of unrequited love comically and both consist of four stanzas of eight alternately rhymed lines.

Title: the Rowley Mile is a race-course on Newmarket Heath in England.

Cyrano de Bergerac

First publication and source text: the *Bell* (January 1954).

Title: the poem is based on the celebrated five-act verse drama of the same title by Edmond Rostand, first produced in 1898. In the play the eponymous hero's large nose proves a romantic impediment. Reviewing a film version of this play in 1952, Kavanagh commented that Cyrano's disability was 'a symbol of the price by which every gift is bought' (*Kavanagh's Weekly*, 21 June 1952).

Intimate Parnassus

First publication: the *Bell* (March 1954).

Source text: *Come Dance with Kitty Stobling* (1960).

Title: the *Iliad* refers to Olympus, not Parnassus, as the home of the gods, but Parnassus was Kavanagh's preferred sacred mountain. Parnassus, originally a mountain in central Greece sacred to the Muses, was a rather old-fashioned term for literary inspiration by the 1940s, but it was a favourite with Kavanagh – cf. 'Dear Folks', 'Lines Written on a Seat on the Grand Canal' and 'Temptation in Harvest'. Parnassus is here represented as a height of detachment and condescension.

On Reading a Book on Common Wild Flowers
First publication and source text: the *Bell* (March 1954).
Sow thistle, fleabane, saxifrage and gentian are common wild flowers.

Narcissus and the Women
First publication and source text: the *Bell* (March 1954).
Title: in Ovid's *Metamorphoses*, Narcissus who falls in love with his own reflection is desired by only one woman, Echo, whereas the hero of this poem is the object of many women's attention.

Irish Stew
First publication and source text: the *Bell* (July 1954).
Title: Irish stew is a national dish whose ingredients include mutton and potatoes.
The Irish politician satirized in this monologue is probably Frank Aiken who, as Minister for External Affairs, had intervened in 1951 to veto the Cultural Relations Committee's recommendation that Kavanagh be sent to give readings of his work in the USA. This would appear to have been the first occasion that the Minister turned down a recommendation by the Committee, which had been established in January 1949 to advise on the expenditure of public money in the promotion of Irish culture in other countries.
Cork is the name of an Irish city and county; 'O'Leary' is a common surname.
Clongowes Wood College is a well-known Jesuit boarding-school in County Kildare, founded in 1814.

Kerry is an Irish county; Naas is a town in County Kildare; Clonakilty is a town in County Cork.

Beniamino Gigli (1890–1957) was an internationally famous Italian tenor who sang at the Metropolitan Opera House in New York and at Covent Garden.

Rainier Maria Rilke (1875–1926), one of the leading German language poets, is most famous for the *Duino Elegies* and the *Sonnets to Orpheus*.

Prelude

First publication: the *Irish Times* (12 February 1955) as 'From a Prelude'.

Source text: *Come Dance with Kitty Stobling* (1960).

Title: may allude to William Wordsworth's autobiographical epic *The Prelude* (1850).

Stanza 1. Apollo, the sun god of the Greeks and Romans, and patron of music and poetry, was often represented as an 'archer', armed with bow and arrow. There is an allusion to the barbed nature of much of Kavanagh's recent satiric poetry.

'comic spirit'. Comedy was to be the poet's preferred aesthetic mode after 1955, but he had embraced it as early as *Tarry Flynn* (1948).

'Silence, exile, and cunning' are the 'only arms' that Stephen Dedalus allows himself for his 'defence' in Joyce's *A Portrait of the Artist as a Young Man* (1916).

Stanza 3. The first six lines were omitted in the first published version.

The principal 'art committee' in Ireland in 1955 was the Arts Council, established in 1951.

Stanza 4. 'Inland' may refer to interiority or to a return to Inniskeen.

A millstone is a heavy or crushing burden; the star was a frequent image in Kavanagh's early poetry, used to indicate the beautiful and remote.

Stanza 6. 'Resolution' in the face of 'destitution' may refer to Wordsworth's poem 'Resolution and Independence' (1807).

Stanza 8. 'Tiger burning / In the forest . . .' alludes to William Blake's poem 'The Tyger' (1794), which begins 'Tyger! Tyger! burning bright / In the forests of the night . . .' Blake's forest is here transformed into a psychic state of repose and contentment and Kavanagh's 'gentle tiger' recalls Blake's lamb.

'That Promised Land' was the land of Canaan which God promised to Abraham and his descendants in the Old Testament.

Though the powerful are excommunicated as heretics in the concluding lines, the poem was sent as a Christmas gift in 1954 to John A. Costello, who had been counsel for the defence in Kavanagh's libel action (see note on 'Ninety Fifty-Four' below) the previous spring and was now the Irish Taoiseach. Costello used his considerable influence to obtain an extra-mural lectureship for Kavanagh at University College, Dublin.

Nineteen Fifty-Four

First publication: *Nimbus* (summer 1956). Untitled.

Source text: *Come Dance with Kitty Stobling* (1960).

Title: on 3 February 1954 Kavanagh began a high court action against the *Leinster Leader*, and its printers, claiming that he had been libelled in an article entitled 'Profile: Mr Patrick Kavanagh' published on 11 October 1952. He lost the case but an appeal was granted on 4 March 1955, and on 23 May 1955 the court was informed that the case had been settled. Kavanagh was very distressed by the initial outcome of his libel action. He was also in poor health in 1954, suffering from a cancer of the lung which was not diagnosed until March 1955.

The Hospital

First publication: *Nimbus* (winter 1956).

Source text: *Come Dance with Kitty Stobling* (1960).

This issue of *Nimbus* included a mini-collection of Kavanagh's previously uncollected poetry, nineteen poems in all, with an introductory essay by Anthony Cronin, 'Innocence and Experi-

ence: The Poetry of Patrick Kavanagh'. It also included a por-
trait of Kavanagh by his Irish painter friend Patrick Swift, who
had sent the poems to *Nimbus*. The *Nimbus* collection was seen
by the poetry reader for Longmans, Thomas Blackburn, and
led to the publication of *Come Dance with Kitty Stobling* in 1960
(see *PS . . . of course, Patrick Swift, 1927–1983*, ed. Veronica Jane
O'Mara, Cork, 1993, pp. 180–81).

The Rialto Hospital in Dublin where Kavanagh was operated on
for lung cancer in March 1955 has since been closed down. The
poem was originally entitled 'April 1956' (Kav/B/48, Kavanagh
Archive, University College, Dublin).

Leaves of Grass

First publication and source text: *Time and Tide* (1 December 1956).

Title: though Walt Whitman's poetry is disparaged in l. 12, the
title of this poem is the same as that of his lengthy poetic master-
piece (1855).

'an idiot boy' is an allusion to Wordsworth's poem 'The Idiot Boy'
(1798), where the boy's mother, Betty Foy, is much concerned
about his welfare.

'Cleopatra's variety'. In Shakespeare's *Antony and Cleopatra* (II. ii),
Enobarbus famously says of Cleopatra that 'Age cannot wither
her, nor custom stale / Her infinite variety . . .'

Bachelor's Walk is a street in Dublin.

October

First publication: *Encounter* (January 1958).
Source text: *Come Dance with Kitty Stobling* (1960).

Requiem for a Mill

First publication: *Studies* (spring 1958).
Source text: *Come Dance with Kitty Stobling* (1960).

Title: the closing-down of Carolan's corn-mill in Inniskeen
prompted this poem; there is an allusion to death in many of
Kavanagh's later 1950s poems.

'pollard' is a type of bran.

Birth

First publication and source text: *Studies* (spring 1958).

Title: Kavanagh claimed that he had been born or reborn as a poet on the banks of Dublin's Grand Canal between the Baggot Street and Leeson Street bridges in July 1955. It was a warm summer and he was convalescing out of doors following an operation for lung cancer. (See *Self-Portrait*, 1964, and note on 'The Hospital' above.)

Question to Life

First publication: *Time and Tide* (12 April 1958).

Source text: *Come Dance with Kitty Stobling* (1960).

More low-key than Kavanagh's customary approach to the theme of love of nature – cf. 'Innocence', 'Miss Universe' and 'Temptation in Harvest'.

The 'primrose banks' may refer to the 1939 sonnet 'Primrose', whose child-seer is seated on a primrose bank.

Come Dance with Kitty Stobling

First publication: *Encounter* (May 1958) as 'High Journey'.

Source text: *Come Dance with Kitty Stobling* (1960).

Title: Kitty Stobling is an invented name for the poet's muse. The original title drew attention to the poem's resemblance to Yeats's 'High Talk' (1938), where Malachi Stilt-Jack stalking on 'timber-toes' is a figure of the poet.

Kavanagh moved through 'colourful country' to arrive at this poem on its second publication in *Nonplus* (October 1959) where it closed a sequence of poetry and prose which included 'three coloured sonnets' (see note on 'Yellow Vestment' below).

Is

First publication: *Encounter* (May 1958).

Source text: *Come Dance with Kitty Stobling* (1960).

To Hell with Commonsense

First publication: *Encounter* (May 1958).

Source text: *Come Dance with Kitty Stobling* (1960).

'All hope abandon, ye who enter here' is inscribed upon the lintel of the gate of Hell in Dante's *Inferno*, Canto III.

'the final Wake Up' is an allusion to the description of the Last Judgement in the New Testament Book of Revelation as a time when all the dead will come to life.

Canal Bank Walk

First publication: *Encounter* (May 1958).

Source text: *Come Dance with Kitty Stobling* (1960).

Title: see note on 'Birth' above.

In the first two lines of this sonnet the imagery is baptismal.

'Word'. Kavanagh connects divine and poetic expression through this allusion to St John 1:1.

Dear Folks

First publication: the *Irish Times* (12 July 1958).

Source text: *Come Dance with Kitty Stobling* (1960).

Title: if one includes the title and signature, this sonnet takes the form of a letter to the poet's readers.

'I lived in the name of a nation' refers to Kavanagh's early acquiescence in Literary Revival ethnicity which he vehemently repudiated in the 1950s.

The 'documents' may be his own satires, but are more likely to refer to others' uncomplimentary views on him as man and poet.

'To walk Parnassus' is 'to write poetry'. (See note on 'Intimate Parnassus' above.)

Song at Fifty

First publication: *Recent Poems* (1958). Limited edition.

First journal publication: *The Times Literary Supplement* (19 December 1958).

Source text: *Come Dance with Kitty Stobling* (1960).

Title: Kavanagh was actually fifty-four in 1958.

This poem might be compared with 'Auditors In', where financial imagery was deployed in a negative account of the poet's career.

'stride across the world' recalls the fantastic and exuberant journey in 'Come Dance with Kitty Stobling'. The 'knight' had already appeared as a self-image in the short story 'The Lay of the Crooked Knight' (1946).

Freedom

First publication: *Recent Poems* (1958). Limited edition.

First journal publication: *Nonplus* (October 1959). Untitled.

Source text: *Come Dance with Kitty Stobling* (1960).

In *Nonplus* the poem opens a sequence of prose and poetry which concludes with 'Come Dance with Kitty Stobling'.

Mount Olympus in northern Thessaly was the fabled dwelling-place of the greater gods in Greek mythology.

'People who are unsure of themselves cannot afford to break out into uproarious laughter or use a piece of slang,' Kavanagh wrote (*Studies*, spring 1959), and 'the main feature about a poet . . . is his humourosity' (*Self-Portrait*, 1964).

Lines Written on a Seat on the Grand Canal, Dublin

First publication: *Recent Poems* (1958). Limited edition.

First journal publication: *Studies* (spring 1959).

Source text: *Come Dance with Kitty Stobling* (1960).

Title: see note on 'Birth' above. A bench in Kavanagh's memory erected on the bank of the Grand Canal at the fourth lock near Mespil Road was unveiled on St Patrick's Day, 1968. A bronze sculpture by John Coll of Kavanagh sitting on a bench, erected nearby, was unveiled on 11 June 1991.

'niagarously' is a comically inflationary neologism based on the Niagara Falls.

The 'barge' is as 'fantastic' as the light in the previous line; though there was a branch line of the Grand Canal connecting with Athy in County Kildare, there was no commercial traffic on the canal by summer 1955.

The reference to 'swan' and 'mythologies' may be a deliberate recollection of Yeatsian motifs; the collocation of 'tomb' and 'passer-by' recalls the closing line of the verse on Yeats's head-stone, 'Horseman pass by.'

The Self-Slaved

First publication: *Recent Poems* (1958). Limited edition.
First journal publication: *Studies* (spring 1959).
Source text: *Come Dance with Kitty Stobling* (1960).
'the grand tour'. The prolonged visit to continental Europe which was considered a desirable feature of a gentleman's education in the eighteenth and nineteenth centuries. Kavanagh had visited North America for approximately five months in 1956/7 and, thereafter, began using travel as an image of liberation – cf. 'Song at Fifty'.
Commenting on a variant version of two lines of this poem ('The main thing is to be free / From self-necessity'), Kavanagh wrote: 'I discovered that the important thing above all was to avoid taking oneself sickly seriously. One of the good ways of getting out of this respectability is the judicious use of slang and of outrageous rhyming' (*Studies*, spring 1959).
'Throw away thy sloth . . . wrath'. Based on the opening stanza of 'Discipline' (1633) by George Herbert:

> Throw away thy rod,
> Throw away thy wrath:
> O my God,
> Take the gentle path.

Prometheus. See note on 'Yellow Vestment' below. Prometheus was the hero of Aeschylus' *Prometheus Bound*. His liberation from captivity was celebrated by Shelley in the poetic drama *Prometheus Unbound* (1820), and it is the freed Prometheus who summons the speaker in this poem.

The One

First publication: *Recent Poems* (1958). Limited edition.
First journal publication: *Nonplus* (October 1959). Untitled.

Source text: *Come Dance with Kitty Stobling* (1960).

The rhyming of 'red' with 'incred' and 'God' with 'bog' are instances of the 'outrageous rhyming' which Kavanagh was cultivating in the late 1950s. (See note on 'The Self-Slaved' above and on 'Yellow Vestment' below.)

'anonymous'. Like many country-bred people, the speaker knows only a few species of wild flower by name.

Yellow Vestment

First publication: *Recent Poems* (1958). Limited edition

First journal publication: *Nonplus* (October 1959). Untitled.

Source text: *Come Dance with Kitty Stobling* (1960).

Title: vestments, which are ceremonial garments worn by Roman Catholic priests when performing certain religious rites, are colour-coded in accordance with ecclesiastical seasons and feasts. Yellow or gold is the most versatile, since it can be substituted for white (Christmas, Easter and major feastdays), for red (feasts of martyrs) and for green (most Sundays that fall outside Advent and Lent). The poet persona dons a cloak of gold in 'Song at Fifty'. In *Nonplus* this sonnet was the first of a sequence of three which were numbered and described as 'three coloured sonnets'; the other two were 'Miss Universe' and 'The One'.

'Prometheus'. In Greek mythology he was a demi-god who stole fire from Olympus and taught men to use it, for which Zeus punished him by chaining him to a rock in the Caucasus, where his liver was preyed upon daily by a vulture.

'Chinese deity' is probably Buddha who, though he was an historic figure, was regarded as a god by many of his less enlightened followers.

'folk song' in l. 6 was changed to 'fold song' in *Come Dance with Kitty Stobling*, a misprint.

A roundelay is a short, simple song with a refrain, such as is often found in folk song. The last line originally read: 'And wear your certainty like a monkish habit.'

Love in a Meadow
First publication: *Recent Poems* (1958). Limited edition.
First journal publication: *Nonplus* (October 1959). Untitled.
Source text: *Come Dance with Kitty Stobling* (1960).

Toprass is an Inniskeen place-name, chosen because it suggests eminence; there may also be a hint of moral high ground. Kavanagh was actually born in Mucker, which means 'place of pigs'. He was obsessed with images of birth and rebirth in the late 1950s – cf. note on 'Birth'.

Miss Universe
First publication: *Recent Poems* (1958). Limited edition.
First journal publication: *Nonplus* (October 1959). Untitled.
Source text: *Come Dance with Kitty Stobling* (1960).

Title: Kavanagh, who often personified the country as female, here updates the image by invoking the context of the beauty competition. (See also note on 'Yellow Vestment' above.)
The five wise virgins in St Matthew 25: 1–13 provided themselves with oil for their lamps and were ready to go to the wedding feast when the bridegroom arrived unexpectedly at midnight; the five unwise virgins who had to go in search of oil were late for the feast and were locked out.

Winter
First publication: *Nonplus* (October 1959).
Source text: *Come Dance with Kitty Stobling* (1960).

Living in the Country
First publication and source text: *X*, vol.1, no.1 (November 1959).
In *Collected Poems* (1964) this was presented as the first part of a two-part poem: the *X* text was 'Living in the Country: I' and 'The Poet's Ready Reckoner' (*Arena*, autumn 1963) was 'Living in the Country: II'. The poem's perspective on country life is corroborated in some of Kavanagh's contemporary comments

on Inniskeen in his letters, e.g. 'Inniskeen is OK for health of body but awful otherwise. Socially plain hell' (letter of 30 January 1960, *Lapped Furrows*, ed. Peter Kavanagh, New York, 1969).

In the *Iliad*, Briseis, a woman captured by Achilles as a prize of war, is claimed by Agamemnon and taken into his tent. Compelled to surrender Briseis, Achilles refuses to take any further part in the Trojan war until she has been returned to him.

In many Irish Catholic families it was customary to recite the rosary aloud in the evenings and to follow it with a number of short prayers for special favours, known as the 'trimmings of the rosary'. The 'trimmings' are the 'glossary' Kavanagh refers to here.

News Item

First publication and source text: the *Observer* (20 November 1960).

'Tom ... eyed'. The allusion is to a poem by Thomas Hood of 1827 which begins:

> I remember, I remember
> The house where I was born
> The little window where the sun
> Came peeping in at morn ...

In William Cowper's comic poem 'The Diverting History of John Gilpin' (1782), John Gilpin, a linen-draper 'of famous London town', is persuaded by his wife to celebrate their twentieth wedding anniversary and follows the family party on a borrowed horse. The horse bolts and most of the poem is devoted to describing Gilpin's misadventures on the runaway. 'Malted' means 'drunk' here; Gilpin was sober and the two large flagons of wine he was carrying for the family celebration were broken on the journey.

Paul Potts (1911–90), poet and critic, had a flat in Islington from which he habitually walked each day to the West End. He wrote admiringly of Kavanagh in his autobiography, *Dante Called You Beatrice* (1960), and in several articles.

Kavanagh had known the poet and architectural historian John Betjeman in Dublin in the early 1940s (see note on 'I Had a Future' above). Betjeman's *Collins Guide to English Parish Churches* (London, 1958) is alluded to here.

Kavanagh occasionally resided at 47 Gibson Square, London, between 1961 and 1964.

Charles Dickens (1812–1870) probably receives a mention as the novelist most famously associated with London.

Mermaid Tavern

First publication and source text: *X* (July 1962).

Title: Kavanagh was an alcoholic in the 1960s and many of his later poems include references to public-houses and to alcoholism; here he summons up a longstanding association between literary culture and pub culture. The Mermaid Tavern at 29–30 Bread Street, London, was famous as the meeting-place of the Friday Street Club (sometimes known as the Mermaid Club) founded by Sir Walter Raleigh. Members included Shakespeare, John Donne and Ben Jonson. Keats also wrote 'Lines on the Mermaid Tavern' (1820):

> Souls of poets dead and gone
> What Elysium have ye known,
> Happy fields or mossy cavern
> Choicer than the Mermaid Tavern.

Ernest Hemingway (1899–1961) projected an image of himself as a tough 'hunting, shooting and fishing' type; he went on several safari trips and wrote about this in *The Green Hills of Africa* (1935) and most memorably in two stories, 'The Short Happy Life of Francis Macomber' and 'The Snows of Kilimanjaro' (both 1936).

'Beckett's garbage-can' alludes to *Endgame* (1958) by Samuel

Beckett in which two characters, Nagg and Nell, are each con-
fined to an ashbin for the duration of the play. Kavanagh is
reputed to have attended at least a dozen performances of *Wait-
ing for Godot* at the Pike Theatre in London in 1955 and further
performances at the Gate Theatre in Dublin in 1956 (see *PS . . .
of course, Patrick Swift, 1927–1983*, ed. Veronica Jane O'Mara,
Cork, 1993, p. 60). He published 'Some Reflections on *Waiting
for Godot,* in the *Irish Times* (28 January 1956).

Literary Adventures

First publication and source text: *Poetry Ireland* (autumn 1962).

John Jordan (1930–88), a Dublin poet, short-story writer and
academic, was a friend of Kavanagh's. He was editor of *Poetry
Ireland* in 1962.

John Lennon was an Inniskeen neighbour.

That Garage

First publication and source text: *Arena* (spring 1963).

'Georgian' is a term often used pejoratively to characterize a technic-
ally conservative, pastoral poetry popular in England from 1912
to the early 1930s.

Richard Church (1893–1972). A writer and minor English poet,
best known for his two-part autobiography, *Over the Bridge*
(1955), and *The Golden Sovereign* (1957).

Lawrence Binyon (1868–1943). An English art historian and
minor poet, best known for his 1914 poem 'For the Fallen'.

The Same Again

First publication and source text: *Arena* (spring 1963).

Thank You, Thank You

First publication and source text: *Arena* (spring 1963).

At the prompting of the Taoiseach, John A. Costello, Kavanagh
was invited to give a course of ten evening lectures on poetry in
spring 1955 (see note on 'Prelude' above). Kavanagh was ill

with lung cancer in spring 1955, so the lectures did not begin until the following year. They proved so successful that they were repeated for a number of years. The Arts Council considered publishing the lectures under the title *The Forgiven Plough*, but the scheme was abandoned.

'on the shelf'. Kavanagh was still a bachelor in 1963; he married Katherine Barry Maloney on 19 April 1967.

The Appian Way was the ancient high road from Rome to Campania and south Italy, constructed in 312 BC. It is also the name of a Dublin road.

In Blinking Blankness: Three Efforts

First publication and source text: *Arena* (spring 1963).

Walter Lowenfels (1897–1976) was a North American poet who published some poetry in the *Irish Statesman*, the first literary and cultural journal Kavanagh ever read. His collection *Finale of Seem* (1929) was known to the Dublin literary set with whom Kavanagh became acquainted in the early 1930s (see Introduction).

'the wren got caught in the furze'.: It was a St Stephen's Day (Boxing Day) custom in parts of rural Ireland for groups of youths, known as 'wren-boys', to call at neighbours' houses, collecting money. Originally, they would have carried a dead wren. The verse or verses they recited varied from place to place; the Inniskeen version was:

> The wren, the wren, the king of all birds,
> On St Stephen's Day he got caught in the furze,
> Although he was little, his fame it was great,
> So get up Mrs——, and give us a treat.

The 'wren' and the 'eagle turned turkey' (turned turtle) both allude to the killing of a regal bird at Christmastime, but do so comically.

One Wet Summer

Source text: *Collected Poems* (1964).

An Insult

First publication and source text: the *New Statesman* (21 February 1964).

'Yeats's dream great house' alludes to his poem 'The Curse of Cromwell' (1937).

Personal Problem

First publication and source text: *Arena* (spring 1965).

Kavanagh implicitly compares his poetry with Yeats's in this poem. Throughout his career, with the recurring figure of Cuchulain, Yeats had drawn on the Gaelic Tain cycle ('old saga') which is based on a quarrel over cattle. He was attracted to Indian mysticism in the early and late phases of his career, and the 'Hindu scale' probably refers to his collaboration with Shri Purohit Swami in a translation of *The Ten Principal Upanishads* in 1935–6.

Glossary of Farming Terms

cattle-drovers   cattle-dealers.

check-rein   in a team of horses, the rein that attaches one horse's head to the other.

coltsfoot   a weed that spreads easily in the fields and is difficult to eradicate.

coulter   part of a plough – the iron blade fixed in front of the ploughshare.

double-tree   a wooden bar, a few feet long, used in ploughing with a team of horses; the two ends were attached to the two horses and the middle was attached to the plough.

drag   see under *scraw-knife* below.

drain   a deep channel in a field to carry off water.

drill   both the furrow in which vegetables are sown or planted and the row of plants.

drilling-bar   a wooden bar similar in shape and function to a *double-tree* (see above), but longer.

fair-green   a site, often near the centre of a town, where animals were bought and sold and entertainments held.

graip   pronged implement used for digging; also to dig using this implement.

gripe   a small open ditch or trench.

haggard   part of a farmyard where straw and hay are stored.

harrow   horse-drawn implement with iron teeth for breaking clods on ploughed land or covering newly sown seed.

headland   strip of unploughed land at both ends of a ploughed field where the horses turned when ploughing.

hunter-hoe   a horse-drawn implement for loosening the soil or scraping up weeds.

lea-field/green   grassland.

mandril   part of a plough.

potato-pit trench in which potatoes were stored covered with earth and straw to protect them from the frost.

rick large stack of hay or corn, especially one built in a rectangular shape.

saddle-harrow a saddle-shaped harrow, lighter than a normal *harrow* (see above), used to turn over the surface soil.

scraw-knife and drag scraw is a thin covering of grass-covered soil that forms upon the surface of a *drain* (see above); a drag is a hook-like implement used to remove the scraw once it has been cut with a scraw-knife.

spavined used of a horse that has a distended hock-joint.

straddle part of a horse's or donkey's harness. It is also used as a verb meaning 'to put the straddle on' the horse or donkey.

the threshing harvest occasion when the farmer hired a threshing-machine which separated the grain from the straw. Neighbours were hired to help or offered their services in return for help on their own threshing day.

traces the chains which connect the horses' harness to the plough.

wild shoots offshoots, suckers or growths from the main stock, occurring accidentally.

winkers part of a horse's or donkey's harness.

Appendix: Contents of Collections

Ploughman and Other Poems, Macmillan, London, 1936.

Ploughman; To a Blackbird; Mary; I May Reap; The Goat of Slieve Donard; Ascetic; The Intangible; Beech Tree; Soft Ease; A Star; Dark Ireland; To a Child; To a Late Poplar; Dreamer; Gold Watch; Twisted Furrows; Worship; Phoenix; After May; The Chase; Four Birds; Blind Dog; Tinker's Wife; April; To a Child; Inniskeen Road: July Evening; Pioneers; A Wind; At Noon; March; Morning

A Soul for Sale and Other Poems, Macmillan, London, 1947.

Pegasus; Father Mat; Temptation in Harvest; Bluebells for Love; Advent; A Christmas Childhood; Memory of My Father; The Long Garden; Primrose; Art McCooey; Spraying the Potatoes; Ethical; Sanctity; Candida; War and Peace; Stony Grey Soil; Memory of Brother Michael; A Wreath for Tom Moore's Statue; The Great Hunger

Recent Poems, the Peter Kavanagh Hand Press, New York, 1958 (25 copies).

To Hell with Commonsense; Is; Canal Bank; October; Requiem for a Mill; Auditors In; Song at Fifty; Freedom; Dear Folks; Lines Written on a Seat on the Grand Canal, Dublin; The Self-Slaved; The One; Yellow Vestment; Love in a Meadow; High Journey (Come Dance with Kitty Stobling); Miss Universe; Prelude; If Ever You Go To Dublin Town; In Memory of My Mother; Epic

Come Dance with Kitty Stobling, Longmans, Green and Co., London, 1960.

Canal Bank Walk; Lines Written on a Seat on the Grand Canal, Dublin; Is; To Hell with Commonsense; Requiem for a Mill; Auditors In; Song at Fifty; Dear Folks; Freedom; October; The Self-Slaved; The One; Yellow Vestment; Love in a Meadow; Come Dance with Kitty Stobling; Miss Universe; Prelude; If Ever You Go To Dublin Town; In Memory of My Mother; Epic; Winter; Question to Life; To the Man after the Harrow; On Looking into E. V. Rieu's Homer; Kerr's Ass; Intimate Parnassus; Ante-Natal Dream; To Be Dead; Peace; Shancoduff; Nineteen Fifty-Four; The Hospital; The Hero; House Party; The Paddiad

Index of Titles

Address to an Old Wooden Gate 3
Advent 66
After Forty Years of Age 108
After May 5
Ante-Natal Dream 91
Art McCooey 16
Auditors In 97
Ballad, A 105
Bank Holiday 92
Birth 122
Bluebells for Love 74
Canal Bank Walk 126
Christmas Childhood, A 14
Come Dance with Kitty Stobling 123
Consider the Grass Growing 67
Cyrano de Bergerac 110
Dear Folks 126
Epic 101
Father Mat 77
Freedom 128
God in Woman 103
Great Hunger, The 18
Having Confessed 106
Hired Boy, The 7
Hospital, The 119
I Had a Future 104
If Ever You Go To Dublin Town 106
In Blinking Blankness: Three Efforts 142
In Memory of My Mother 82
Inniskeen Road: July Evening 6
Innocence 101
Insult, An 144
Intimate Parnassus 112
Irish Poets Open Your Eyes 94

Irish Stew	114
Is	124
Kerr's Ass	95
Leaves of Grass	119
Lines Written on a Seat on the Grand Canal, Dublin	129
Literary Adventures	138
Living in the Country	134
Long Garden, The	17
Lough Derg	45
Love in a Meadow	132
Memory of Brother Michael	73
Memory of My Father	10
Mermaid Tavern	137
Miss Universe	132
Narcissus and the Women	113
News Item	136
Nineteen Fifty-Four	118
No Social Conscience	84
October	120
On Looking into E. V. Rieu's Homer	102
On Raglan Road	83
On Reading a Book on Common Wild Flowers	113
One, The	131
One Wet Summer	144
Paddiad, The	85
Peace	68
Pegasus	71
Personal Problem	145
Plough-Horses	9
Ploughman	4
Poplar Memory	8
Prelude	115
Pygmalion	4
Question to Life	122
Requiem for a Mill	121
Rowley Mile, The	109
Same Again, The	140
Sanctity	7

Self-Slaved, The	129
Shancoduff	8
Snail	9
Song at Fifty	127
Spraying the Potatoes	11
Spring Day	90
Stony Grey Soil	13
Temptation in Harvest	75
Thank You, Thank You	141
That Garage	140
Threshing Morning	68
Tinker's Wife	5
To Be Dead	94
To Hell with Commonsense	125
To the Man After the Harrow	11
Wet Evening in April	105
Who Killed James Joyce?	96
Winter	133
Wreath for Tom Moore's Statue, A	70
Yellow Vestment	131

Index of First Lines

A poplar leaf was spiked upon a thorn   75
A year ago I fell in love with the functional ward   119
And sometimes I am sorry when the grass   68
Another summer, another July   144
As I was walking down a street   109
Battered by time and weather; scarcely fit   3
Christmas, someone mentioned, is almost upon us   133
Clay is the word and clay is the flesh   18
Consider the grass growing   67
Every old man I see   10
From Cavan and from Leitrim and from Mayo   45
Give us another poem, he said   115
Green, blue, yellow and red –   131
Having confessed he feels   106
He was an egoist with an unsocial conscience   84
I am here all morning with the familiar   142
I am here in a garage in Monaghan.   138
I came to a great house on the edge of a park   144
I do not think of you lying in the wet clay   82
I go from you, I recede   9
I have lived in important places, times   101
I have my friends, my public and they are waiting   140
I learned, I learned – when one might be inclined   132
I only know that I was there   91
I recover now the time I drove   16
I saw her amid the dunghill debris   5
I saw her in a field, a stone-proud woman   4
I turn the lea-green down   4
I walked under the autumned poplars that my
    father planted   8
If ever you go to Dublin town   106
In a meadow   77
In Islington for the moment I reside   136
In the corner of a Dublin pub   85

Irish poets open your eyes   94
It came as a pleasant surprise   127
It was the garden of the golden apples   17
It was the Warm Summer, that landmark   134
It would never be morning, always evening   73
Just a line to remind my friends that after much trouble   126
Lately I have been travelling by a created guidance   131
Leafy-with-love banks and the green waters of the canal   126
Let me be no wiser than the dull   7
Like Achilles you had a goddess for mother,   102
Many women circled the prison of Reflection   113
May came, and every shabby phoenix flapped   5
Me I will throw away.   129
Men are what they are, and what they do   112
More kicks than pence   125
My black hills have never seen the sun rising   8
My soul was an old horse   71
Nineteen-fifty was the year   92
Nineteen Fifty-Four hold on till I try   118
No, no, no, I know I was not important as I moved   123
No System, no Plan,   137
Now I must search till I have found my God –   103
Now leave the check-reins slack,   11
O Come all ye tragic poets and sing a stave with me –   90
O commemorate me where there is water   129
O cruel are the women of Dublin's fair city   105
O I had a future   104
O leafy yellowness you create for me   120
O stony grey soil of Monaghan   13
O the prickly sow thistle that grew in the hollow
   of the Near Field   113
On an apple-ripe September morning   68
On Raglan Road on an autumn day I met her
   first and knew   83
One side of the potato-pits was white with frost –   14
Our ancient civilization – and –   114
. . . Particularly if yourself   141
She kicked a pebble with her toe   110

She waved her body in the circle sign	132
Surely you would not ask me to have known	122
Take me to the top of the high hill	128
The barrels of blue potato-spray	11
The bicycles go by in twos and threes –	6
The birds sang in the wet trees	105
The cowardice of Ireland is in his statue	70
The important thing is not	124
The lilacs by the gate	140
The problem that confronts me here	97
Their glossy flanks and manes outshone	9
There was a time when a mood recaptured was enough	108
There will be bluebells growing under the big trees	74
They laughed at one I loved	101
They took away the water-wheel,	121
To be a poet and not know the trade	7
To be dead is to stop believing in	94
To take something as a subject, indifferent	145
We borrowed the loan of Kerr's big ass	95
We have tested and tasted too much, lover –	66
We will not hold an inquest on the past –	122
When I was growing up and for many years after	119
Who killed James Joyce?	96

PENGUIN ⬤ CLASSICS

- Details about every Penguin Classic

- Advanced information about forthcoming titles

- Hundreds of author biographies

- FREE resources including critical essays on the books and their historical background, reader's and teacher's guides.

- Links to other web resources for the Classics

- Discussion area

- Online review copy ordering for academics

- Competitions with prizes, and challenging Classics trivia quizzes

PENGUIN CLASSICS ONLINE

READ MORE IN PENGUIN

In every corner of the world, on every subject under the sun, Penguin represents quality and variety – the very best in publishing today.

For complete information about books available from Penguin – including Puffins, Penguin Classics and Arkana – and how to order them, write to us at the appropriate address below. Please note that for copyright reasons the selection of books varies from country to country.

In the United Kingdom: Please write to *Dept. EP, Penguin Books Ltd, Bath Road, Harmondsworth, West Drayton, Middlesex UB7 ODA*

In the United States: Please write to *Consumer Sales, Penguin Putnam Inc., P.O. Box 12289 Dept. B, Newark, New Jersey 07101-5289.* VISA and MasterCard holders call 1-800-788-6262 to order Penguin titles

In Canada: Please write to *Penguin Books Canada Ltd, 10 Alcorn Avenue, Suite 300, Toronto, Ontario M4V 3B2*

In Australia: Please write to *Penguin Books Australia Ltd, P.O. Box 257, Ringwood, Victoria 3134*

In New Zealand: Please write to *Penguin Books (NZ) Ltd, Private Bag 102902, North Shore Mail Centre, Auckland 10*

In India: Please write to *Penguin Books India Pvt Ltd, 11 Community Centre, Panchsheel Park, New Delhi 110017*

In the Netherlands: Please write to *Penguin Books Netherlands bv, Postbus 3507, NL-1001 AH Amsterdam*

In Germany: Please write to *Penguin Books Deutschland GmbH, Metzlerstrasse 26, 60594 Frankfurt am Main*

In Spain: Please write to *Penguin Books S. A., Bravo Murillo 19, 1° B, 28015 Madrid*

In Italy: Please write to *Penguin Italia s.r.l., Via Benedetto Croce 2, 20094 Corsico, Milano*

In France: Please write to *Penguin France, Le Carré Wilson, 62 rue Benjamin Baillaud, 31500 Toulouse*

In Japan: Please write to *Penguin Books Japan Ltd, Kaneko Building, 2-3-25 Koraku, Bunkyo-Ku, Tokyo 112*

In South Africa: Please write to *Penguin Books South Africa (Pty) Ltd, Private Bag X14, Parkview, 2122 Johannesburg*

READ MORE IN PENGUIN

Published or forthcoming:

Ulysses   James Joyce

Written over a seven-year period, from 1914 to 1921, *Ulysses* has survived bowdlerization, legal action and bitter controversy. An undisputed modernist classic, its ceaseless verbal inventiveness and astonishingly wide-ranging allusions confirm its standing as an imperishable monument to the human condition. 'Everybody knows now that *Ulysses* is the greatest novel of the century'   Anthony Burgess, *Observer*

Nineteen Eighty-Four   George Orwell

Hidden away in the Record Department of the Ministry of Truth, Winston Smith skilfully rewrites the past to suit the needs of the Party. Yet he inwardly rebels against the totalitarian world he lives in, which controls him through the all-seeing eye of Big Brother. 'His final masterpiece ... *Nineteen Eighty-Four* is enthralling' Timothy Garton Ash, *New York Review of Books*

The Day of the Locust *and* **The Dream Life of Balso Snell**
Nathanael West

These two novellas demonstrate the fragility of the American dream. In *The Day of the Locust*, talented young artist Todd Hackett has been brought to Hollywood to work in a major studio. He discovers a surreal world of tarnished dreams, where violence and hysteria lurk behind the glittering façade. 'The best of the Hollywood novels, a nightmare vision of humanity destroyed by its obsession with film' J. G. Ballard, *Sunday Times*

The Myth of Sisyphus   Albert Camus

The Myth of Sisyphus is one of the most profound philosophical statements written this century. It is a discussion of the central idea of absurdity that Camus was to develop in his novel *The Outsider*. Here Camus poses the fundamental question – Is life worth living? – and movingly argues for an acceptance of reality that encompasses revolt, passion and, above all, liberty.

READ MORE IN PENGUIN

Published or forthcoming:

Seven Pillars of Wisdom   T. E. Lawrence

Although 'continually and bitterly ashamed' that the Arabs had risen in revolt against the Turks as a result of fraudulent British promises, Lawrence led them in a triumphant campaign. *Seven Pillars of Wisdom* recreates epic events with extraordinary vividness. However flawed, Lawrence is one of the twentieth century's most fascinating figures. This is the greatest monument to his character.

A Month in the Country   J. L. Carr

A damaged survivor of the First World War, Tom Birkin finds refuge in the village church of Oxgodby where he is to spend the summer uncovering a huge medieval wall-painting. Immersed in the peace of the countryside and the unchanging rhythms of village life, Birkin experiences a sense of renewal. Now an old man, he looks back on that idyllic summer of 1920.

Lucky Jim   Kingsley Amis

Jim Dixon has accidentally fallen into a job at one of Britain's new redbrick universities. A moderately successful future beckons, as long as he can survive a madrigal-singing weekend at Professor Welch's, deliver a lecture on 'Merrie England' and resist Christine, the hopelessly desirable girlfriend of Welch's awful son Bertrand. 'A flawless comic novel . . . It has always made me laugh out loud' Helen Dunmore, *The Times*

Under Milk Wood   Dylan Thomas

As the inhabitants of Llareggub lie sleeping, their dreams and fantasies deliciously unfold. Waking up, their dreams turn to bustling activity as a new day begins. In this classic modern pastoral, the 'dismays and rainbows' of the imagined seaside town become, within the cycle of one day, 'a greenleaved sermon on the innocence of men'.

BY THE SAME AUTHOR

Tarry Flynn

A man's mother can be a terrible burden sometimes. For Tarry Flynn – poet, farmer and lover-from-afar of beautiful young virgins – the responsibility of family, farm, poetic inspiration and his own unyeilding lust is a heavy one. The only solution is to rise above it all – or escape over the nearest horizon.

'Any man who wrote *Tarry Flynn* is entitled to throw down his hat and offer a challenge to the wide world. *Tarry Flynn* is a work of art' *Irish Times*

The Green Fool

First published in 1938, *The Green Fool* was withdrawn as a result of a libel action. It is one of those rare books that is difficult to describe with restraint, an autobiography that paints a fascinating picture of a young man in a patriarchal society and captures the essence of Irish rural life. There are exquisite descriptions of country fairs, weddings, dances, poaching expeditions, political banditry and religious pilgrimages.

'*The Green Fool* has Traherne's mystic vision; Hemingway's stark simplicity; Thurber's fantastic humour; and it is one of the few authentic accounts of life in Ireland in the twentieth century' *Irish Press*